SHELLS
JEWELS FROM THE SEA

PLATE 1

PLATE 2

PLATE 3

PHOTOGRAPHER'S DEDICATION

For Lily
Her visual and spiritual assistance helped me find the way.

AUTHOR'S DEDICATION

To R. Tucker Abbott
In grateful appreciation for nurturing a childhood interest into a lifelong fascination.

SHELLS
JEWELS FROM THE SEA

M. G. Harasewych

Associate Curator, Invertebrate Zoology
National Museum of Natural History
Smithsonian Institution

Photographs by Murray Alcosser

Preface by Stephen Jay Gould

Alexander Agassiz Professor of Zoology
Museum of Comparative Zoology
Harvard University

William Bledsoe Shell Collection
National Museum of Natural History
Smithsonian Insitution

COURAGE BOOKS
AN IMPRINT OF RUNNING PRESS
PHILADELPHIA • LONDON

This edition first published in the United States in 1991
by Courage Books, an imprint of Running Press Book Publishers.

Text © 1989, 1991 by M. G. Harasewych

Photographs © 1989, 1991 by Murray Alcosser

Preface © 1989, 1991 Stephen Jay Gould

Library of Congress Cataloging-in-Publication Number 91–71591

Harasewych, M. G.
    Shells: jewels from the sea/by M. G. Harasewych: Photographs by Murray Alcosser
    p.   cm.
    ISBN 1–56138–766–5
    I. Shells—Pictorial works. I. Alcosser, Murray, 1937
II. Title
QL404.H37 1989   89–3578
594´.0471´0222 — dc 19   CIP

Created by Nevraumont Publishing Co., Inc., New York

Editor and Art Director: Peter N. Nevraumont
Consulting Editor: Betty Anne Crawford
Book Designer: Mike Rose
Jacket Designer: Toby Schmidt

Printed in Hong Kong

Published by Courage Books, an imprint of
Running Press Book Publishers,
125 South Twenty-second Street,
Philadelphia, Pennsylvania 19103–4399

Plates 1 and 2 [*preceding pages*]

Entemnotrochus adansonianus (Fischer and Crosse, 1861)
ADANSON'S SLIT SHELL
Western Atlantic Ocean from Bermuda to Brazil
4 to 8 inches (10 to 20 cm)

Plate 3

Coluzea juliae Harasewych, 1989
JULIA'S PAGODA SHELL
Southeastern Africa
3 to 4 inches (7.5 to 10 cm)

Plate 4

Spondylus americanus Hermann, 1781
AMERICAN THORNY OYSTER
Carolinas to Brazil
3 to 4 inches (7.5 to 10 cm.) excluding spines

TABLE OF CONTENTS

PLATE 4

PREFACE

We are always intrigued when two apparently contradictory themes manage to reside in one object or coherent group. Thus, in *Wuthering Heights*, Heathcliff remains one of literature's great characters because we must somehow reconcile his overwhelming and poignant love for Cathy with the cruelty of his behavior.

Boundless diversity and unifying constraint of anatomical design are the two great themes of natural history. They often conflict, as in horseshoe crabs, which have little of the first and much of the second. But these apparently contradictory themes come together in nature's greatest success stories, for the best designs include great flexibility for nearly endless variation upon a basic plan rich in functional utility. The phylum Mollusca, ranking second only to the arthropods in diversity, provides our best example of harmony between the themes of copious variety and common ground plan.

We sense no chaos, or burst of random energy, in the fantastic array of forms displayed in this book, but note instead an underlying order in the central theme of molluscan design—the coiled shell. Some shells are so regular in their growth that they provide, along with the hexagonal cells of honeycombs in hive bees, the finest examples of mathematical regularity in organic form (see, for example, the high-spired genus *Terebra*, plate 160). Indeed, Canon Mosely, an early student of gastropod form, wrote in 1838 about the snail within the shell: "God hath bestowed upon this humble architect the practical skill of a learned geometrician." Several shells bear Latin names that honor this geometric regularity—as *Turritella* (plate 31) or *Architectonica* (plate 34).

But this underlying regularity of coiling also generates the innumerable permutations that define the range of molluscan form, for by varying just a few properties in different ways—the tightness of winding, or the rate of expansion of the tube, for example—nature makes thousands of forms from a single set of rules. Jan Swammerdam, the great 17th century Dutch anatomist, noted: "for all differences, which we admire among them, are generated entirely from the diversity of spirals." We are so attuned to the spiral as a molluscan archetype that our greatest sense of peculiarity or discomfort arises from those few shells that stray from regularity—snails that uncoil (plates 32, 33), clams that reduce the shell to a vestige and calcify an uncoiled feeding or burrowing tube instead (plates 206, 207), or the wondrous genus *Xenophora* (literally the "strange bearer"), which obscures its quite regular coiling by cementing various objects to the shell (plates 43, 44).

The canonical molluscan coil is not of indiscriminate form but a particular type called the logarithmic spiral. Three different styles define the three great groups of mollusks—planispiral for the coiled cephalopods (in a single plane, as in coiling a rope of ever-expanding diameter on a ship's deck), helicospiral (as a cone in three dimensions) for the gastropods (snails), and as two mirror-image coils for the bivalves (clams). Most of the minor molluscan subgroups present further variations—as in the scaphopods (plates 208–210), which coil so gently that their entire shell forms only a fraction of a single coil (leading to their popular name as "elephant tusk" shells).

The older naturalists believed that growth in such mathematical regularity could only represent the direct creative will of a deity, since "lowly" animals could not take square roots or manipulate exponentials. But Darwin and his followers identified natural selection as a mechanism that could produce such regularity by trial and error on a geological scale, as long as the abstract form so evolved provided advantages in the "struggle for life." A bee cannot calculate the angles of a hexagon as an abstract proposition, but the honeycomb provides maximal storage of honey for minimal expenditure in wax. Similarly, the logarithmic spiral has a particular functional property that presumably led to its initial evolution and later stabilization in the Mollusca.

The logarithmic spiral is the only form of coil that increases in size without changing shape. Thus, any organism that grows by coiling (a good way to achieve strength of shell by compactness), and reaches an advantageous shape worth preserving over a large range of size, must take the form of a logarithmic spiral. This curve is therefore a "standard" form in nature, evolved again and again by creatures of no close relationship—as in ram and antelope horns, the shells of some single-celled foraminifera, and even the path of a moth flying towards light.

As a side consequence of its functional role (and not as a primary purpose, as earlier naturalists thought in the hubris of centuries past), the logarithmic spiral tends to evoke a strong sense of aesthetic pleasure in most people. For reasons not well understood, we are attracted to regularity of proportion, and particularly to an even increase that adds coils but does not change the overall shape. D'Arcy Thompson, our greatest student of natural form (see his classic *On Growth and Form*, written in 1917 and still in print), showed how the logarithmic spiral matches the ideal forms of growth that the aestheticians of ancient Greece recognized and designated as the "golden" ratio or section.

The logarithmic spiral may gain its basic explanation as an adaptive form for maintaining shape with compactness in growth. Most of the specialized variations of the spiral are also adaptations to particular modes of life—the thin flattened shells of abalones and limpets (plates 12–16) for clamping to rocks, the exuberant spinosity of murexes for protection (plates 81–102), the streamlined shells of limids for swimming (plate 180). But we mustn't adopt the modern version (evolutionary optimality) of the old myth (created perfection, made by God for us to rule) that filled our forebears with cheer and self-importance, but misconstrued nature so badly. Animals are not incarnations of perfect design, and many basic aspects of form are not built directly by natural selection for some immediate benefit in function. The beautiful and regular color patterns of so many clams (plate 200) and snails (plates 137–140) may have no direct function (and some belong to creatures that live buried in sediment, or that cover their shell with an opaque outer layer of horny material called periostracum); deposition of color may be functional (perhaps only to excrete poisons or waste products), but the actual (and beautiful) patterns may arise only as a side consequence of general rhythms in growth. To take an even more fundamental example, we have no idea why the vast majority of snails coil as righthanded rather than as lefthanded, spirals; the two modes are functionally equivalent as mirror images. (Of more than 150 photos of snails in this book, only plate 117 represents a sinistral, or lefthanded, species.) As D'Arcy Thompson wrote in his incomparable prose: "But why, in the general run of shells, all the world over, in the past and in the present, one direction of twist is so overwhelmingly commoner than the other, no man knows."

If we are intrigued by contrasts in the same objects—unity of form vs. diversity of expression, adaptation vs. side consequences of growth, to cite the two chosen as a basis for this introduction—consider the human division that serves as an ultimate rationale for the collaboration of this book, and for an entire genre of great works in natural history: art vs. science. But here I demur, for the division is false, a product of arbitrary boundaries that arise in an age of intense specialization. Our forebears did not recognize this war of two mutually incomprehensible cultures, this division of beauty and factual knowledge. Agostino Scilla, the great Italian 17th century paleontologist, was primarily a painter. Ernst Haeckel, the leading evolutionist of Germany in Darwin's era, also published one of the great visual works of the *art nouveau* in 1904 (*Kunstformen der Natur*, or Artforms of Nature). We may now need a collaboration or even a team to establish proper unity, but we must recover the integrity that views the work of a photographer and a scientist as parts of a single enterprise. The logarithmic spiral is a marvel of engineering and a work of great beauty. Shells are sources of wonder and sources of knowledge.

Stephen Jay Gould
Cambridge, Massachusetts

INTRODUCTION

It is difficult for anyone to walk along an ocean shore without picking up a shell or two to take home. People of all cultures, from the Paleolithic to the present, have been fascinated by the beauty of shells. Since time immemorial, man has rendered shells or their representations in ornament and adornment. No doubt the factors contributing to their appeal are the diversity of geometric forms and color patterns, combined with size and durability. Actually, shells are the remains of one of the most successful and ancient animal phyla.

A seashell is the external skeleton of a mollusk which, unlike the skeleton of other animals, is composed of one or two sections. Although durable, most animal skeletons become disarticulated into many small pieces when cleaned of flesh. Because of their utility, shells have had considerable influence in molding the aesthetic sense of ancient as well as contemporary cultures.

Curiosity about the process by which shells are formed and the biology of animals that form them is more difficult to date, relying exclusively on written records. Aristotle's *History of Animals* (332 BC) is the oldest surviving work containing references to mollusks. In it, Aristotle makes written observations on the habitats, diets and varieties of many of the more common Mediterranean species of mollusks.

Aristotle's was the first recorded use of the term Mollusca, derived from the Latin *mollis*, meaning soft. Although occasional references to mollusks appeared during the intervening centuries, the earliest work devoted completely to the study of shells is Filippo Buonanni's *Recreation for the Mind and Eye in the Observation of Shelled Animals for Curious Beholders of Nature*, published in Italian (1681) and Latin (1684). Buonanni not only illustrated many of the varieties of shells familiar at the time, including many unique specimens sent to the Collegio Romano from remote regions of the world by Jesuit missionaries, but discussed many of the fundamental questions of his day that related to mollusks. A Jesuit himself, Buonanni justified the study of such "beasts of little account" by noting that the observation of nature elevates the mind toward God, and that man, "in admiring the creatures shall praise the Creator," a view prevalent well into the 19th century. In the light of the knowledge gained in the fields of biology, evolution and genetics during the last three centuries, many of Buonanni's questions or problems (such as whether mollusks are produced sexually or by spontaneous generation) are nonsensical. Many, however, are amazingly insightful. Some, like, "Why can you hear the sea in a shell?" are timeless, familiar to every parent of a young child.

A cursory examination of the photographs in this book suggests a bewildering and seemingly endless variety in the form, sculpture, and color of shells. Closer inspection reveals that the variation is limited, and only a small proportion of possible forms has been exploited. Certain structures and basic designs are recognized as recurring, not only within the diverse phylum Mollusca, but throughout the animal kingdom. Shells may be recognized as structures engineered by nature to meet specific mechanical criteria necessary for the survival of the animal, constrained by raw materials and the rigors of environment as well as by the animal's genetic repertoire.

The beauty of shells is evident. Appreciation of this beauty can only be enhanced by contemplation of the shell's function and the value of its every feature to the animal that produced and inhabited it. The seashells illustrated in this book were chosen not only for their beauty, rarity and perfection, but because many represent landmarks in the courses of evolution of diverse marine molluscan groups. It is hoped that exposition of this beauty of form as well as of design will result in recreation for both mind and eye in present day "curious beholders of nature."

ORIGINS OF THE MOLLUSCAN SHELL

The origin of the phylum Mollusca is ancient and obscure, substantially predating the earliest fossil records, which are 570 million years old. Indeed, most of the nine currently recognized major groups or classes of mollusks had already evolved by the time the oldest fossils were being formed.

Today, knowledge of molluscan evolution is far from complete, and even the relationships of the nine classes are a topic of active current research. Nevertheless, many of the key steps in the evolution of the phylum have been at least tentatively deduced from comparisons of the anatomical organization and embryology of species living today, and corroborated by analyses of the fossil record.

The general consensus is that mollusks evolved from small (0.04–0.08 inch/1–2 mm long), shell-less, flatworm-like ancestors. Like the vast majority of animals including humans, the earliest mollusks were bilaterally symmetrical; that is, could be divided into left and right halves that mirrored each other exactly.

The definitive features of the phylum, including such unique anatomical specializations as the radula (a feeding structure that operates much like a spiked conveyor belt), the mantle (a specialized secretory region on the animal's back), and the mantle cavity (a pouch or infolding of the body wall beneath the mantle that contains respiratory, olfactory, excretory and reproductive organs), became established long before the formation of a shell. However, it was the appearance of a single shell (figure 1) much later in the course of their evolution, that allowed mollusks to exploit new habitats and resulted in a rapid diversification

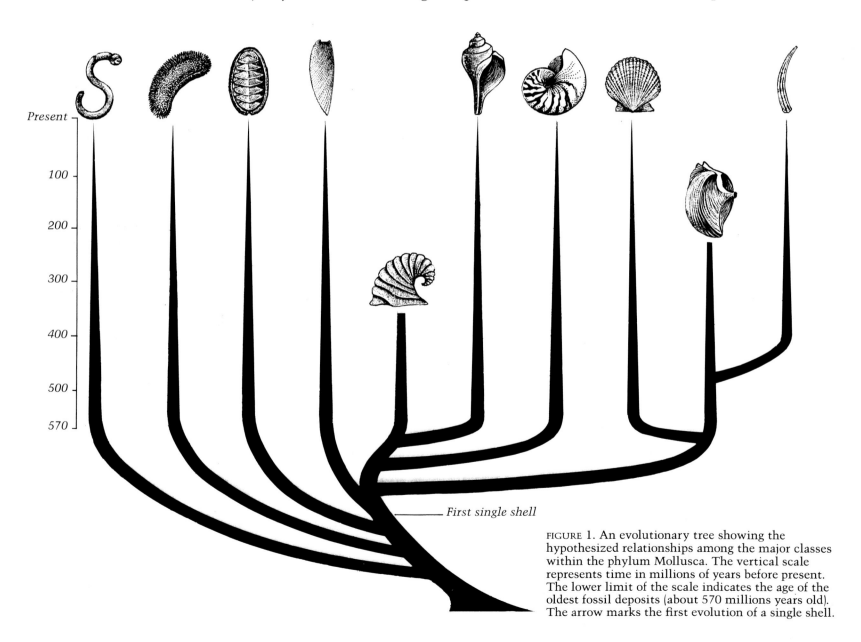

Present —
100 —
200 —
300 —
400 —
500 —
570 —

——— First single shell

FIGURE 1. An evolutionary tree showing the hypothesized relationships among the major classes within the phylum Mollusca. The vertical scale represents time in millions of years before present. The lower limit of the scale indicates the age of the oldest fossil deposits (about 570 millions years old). The arrow marks the first evolution of a single shell.

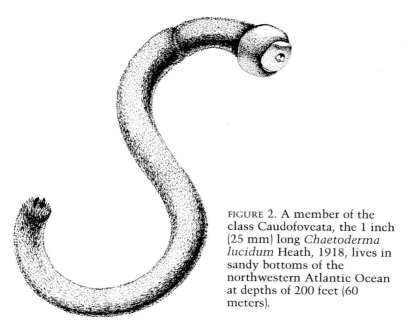

FIGURE 2. A member of the class Caudofoveata, the 1 inch (25 mm) long *Chaetoderma lucidum* Heath, 1918, lives in sandy bottoms of the northwestern Atlantic Ocean at depths of 200 feet (60 meters).

that produced over 98% of the more than 50,000 species living today. Mollusca is second only to the Arthropoda, the phylum that includes insects, in terms of the total number of living species.

The most primitive mollusks living today, the class Caudofoveata (figure 2) represents a lineage that has never evolved a shell. These worm-like animals are covered by a cuticle, a sheet of hair-like protein, in which mineralized scales of calcium carbonate are embedded. Although some species reach nearly six inches (150 mm) in length, most are small (less than 1 inch/25 mm). Caudofoveates burrow in muddy sea bottoms, where they graze on fine sediments rich in organic debris and microscopic organisms.

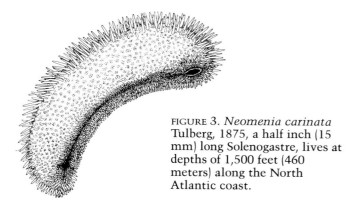

FIGURE 3. *Neomenia carinata* Tulberg, 1875, a half inch (15 mm) long Solenogastre, lives at depths of 1,500 feet (460 meters) along the North Atlantic coast.

Somewhat more advanced are the Solenogastres (figure 3), which are also tubular. These animals are covered along the top and sides by a cuticle containing embedded scales, spicules and spines. Rather than burrowing, Solenogastres crawl along the surface of firmer sea bottoms,

or live and feed on colonies of soft corals. Most are under 1 inch/25 mm long.

Although these two classes are neither diverse nor common, they represent landmarks in the transition of primitive shell-less mollusks from a burrowing to a crawling habitat. The cuticles and scales that aided in burrowing became modified and elaborated to serve a protective function in a more exposed habitat. These spines and scales of calcium carbonate are the forerunners of the molluscan shell.

The chitons (class Polyplacophora, plates 5–8) represent a further stage in the evolution of the calcified molluscan shell. Chitons, still elongate but also flattened, are covered by a shell composed of eight parallel, interlocking rectangular plates surrounded by an elliptical band of proteinaceous cuticle in which spines and scales may be embedded. Each of these calcified plates is thought to have developed through the fusion of a band of scales. Chitons live predominantly on rocks or other hard substrates, and range from areas exposed at low tide to the deep-sea. Most feed on algae, which they scrape off the rocks with their radula. Their jointed shells allow them to conform to uneven surfaces and afford them protection from predators, from drying during exposure at low tide, as well as from mechanical damage by breaking waves. When dislodged, the animals curl like an armadillo or a pill bug, in order to protect their vulnerable fleshy undersides. Their impenetrable and impermeable shell has allowed these mollusks access to new, resource-rich habitats. The development of this type of shell was accompanied by a substantial increase in body size (many species exceed 4 inches/10 cm in length) and diversity (about 600 living species).

It is currently believed that the first single-shelled mollusks (class Monoplacophora) evolved from an early chiton in which the eight shell-secreting regions of the mantle fused to produce a single, continuous shell-secreting gland. Earliest fossil records contain a variety of minute, cap-shaped shells that include two major lineages

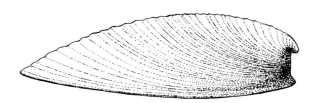

FIGURE 4. Side view of the monoplacophoran *Neopilina galatheae* Lemche, 1957. This species was collected in 11,700 feet (3,570 meters) off the western coast of Mexico.

FIGURE 5. *Latouchella accordionata* Runnegar and Jell, 1976, a minute, coiled monoplacophoran from Middle Cambrian fossil deposits in Australia.

within the Monoplacophora. One lineage, characterized by low, flat shells that extend beyond the animal in all directions (figure 4), survives to the present. These monoplacophorans are known only from a few species that are rarely more than a fraction of an inch long. They inhabit muddy clay bottoms beyond the continental shelves, where they feed on microorganisms and organic matter in the sediment. Although protected by a shell and able to live on the sediment surface, these monoplacophorans probably live much as their protomolluscan ancestors did.

A second monoplacophoran lineage developed more voluminous conical shells that became coiled (figure 5). As the curvature continued to increase, the center of mass shifted forward while the mantle cavity containing respiratory, excretory, and reproductive organs remained at the rear. This lineage, which became extinct some 300 million years ago, is regarded as the progenitor of all the remaining classes of mollusks and of the vast majority of mollusks living today.

Gastropoda (plates 9–163), the most abundant and ecologically diverse of the molluscan classes, evolved from the coiled monoplacophorans. Gastropods are characterized by a developmental process termed torsion. During torsion, which occurs in the larval stages of snails living today, the mantle cavity is rotated from a central, rear-facing position to a forward-facing position. Relocation of the gills and olfactory organs to a forward-facing position directly over the head improved the efficiency of respiration, reduced fouling of the gills by sediment, and enabled snails to use their sense of smell to locate stimuli. Torsion made it possible for the snail to withdraw its head

into its mantle cavity for protection. The resulting shift of the center of gravity to the animal's rear also increased its stability and maneuverability.

Yet torsion was not without disadvantages. Chief among them was the position of excretory and reproductive orifices at the rear of a forward-facing mantle cavity. The need to alter the pattern of water flow and relative position of mantle cavity organs resulted in the loss of anatomical bilateral symmetry, which in turn resulted in asymmetrically coiled shells. This acquired asymmetry, unique to gastropods, is already evident in the earliest fossil records.

When we consider that roughly 70% of all mollusks living today are gastropods, and that snails are the only mollusks to have colonized terrestrial as well as freshwater and marine habitats; we can begin to appreciate the advantages of torsion. Later in the course of gastropod evolution, several advanced lineages have independently reduced anatomical asymmetry, and some have become shell-less.

The vast majority of cephalopods (squids and octopuses) living today are free-swimming and lack an external shell. Yet cephalopods also trace their ancestry to monoplacophorans with tall, conical shells. As the protocephalopod grew, it moved into the expanded, newly secreted region at the opening of the shell and produced partitions or septa to seal off the tighter, upper portions. A series of septa divided the upper region of the shell into chambers that were interconnected by a permeable, tissue-filled tube or siphuncle. Whether these chambers were filled with fluid of decreased salinity or with metabolic gases, they produced some degree of buoyancy that, in time, the animal was able to regulate through the siphuncle.

The transition from a crawling to at least a partially swimming way of life was accompanied by a dramatic series of anatomical and behavioral changes. Tissues surrounding the mouth were modified into tentacles with prehensile or raptorial capabilities. Increased mobility required a higher metabolic rate. Cephalopods developed other features to support this new way of life, among them a predatory diet, more efficient respiratory and circulatory systems, image-forming eyes, and increased speed through the development of jet propulsion. These adaptations allowed cephalopods to exploit a habitat new to mollusks. New varieties and specializations proliferated rapidly.

Of the cephalopods that retained external shells, only the nautiloids have survived to the present day. They are represented by a few species restricted to the genus *Nautilus* (plates 164–165). The rest of the nearly 600 species of cephalopods living today are descended from ancestors that had evolved internal shells.

Based on their development of structurally complex eyes, complex nervous systems, and the ability to learn, cephalopods are regarded by some as the pinnacle of invertebrate evolution. Their numbers include the largest invertebrates that ever lived—there are documented reports of giant squid up to 72 feet (22 meters) in length. Yet, the cephalopods living today represent but a small proportion of the over 10,000 shelled species long extinct and known only from fossil deposits.

Rostroconchia, an extinct class of mollusks, is also believed to have evolved from the tall-shelled monoplacophorans. Rostroconchs are thought to have given rise to Bivalvia, and later to Scaphopoda. Rostroconchs are characterized by having single-valved larval shells and adult shells that appear bivalved (figure 6) due to increased downward growth along both sides of the shell. The resulting laterally compressed shells have deep notches at their front and back ends, and a characteristic internal buttress called a pegma between the valves. The change in shell form from cap-shaped to wedge-shaped must have accompanied a change from the crawling, grazing life style of the monoplacophorans. Early rostroconchs were at

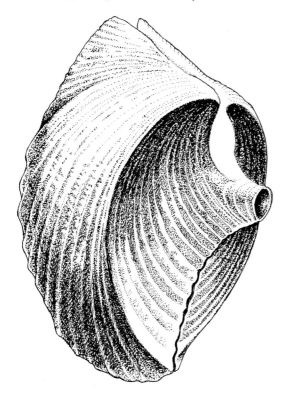

FIGURE 6. *Pseudoconocardium lanterna* (Branson, 1965), a 1 inch (25 mm) long, fossil rostroconch that lived in Texas and Oklahoma during the Late Pennsylvanian.

least partially buried in soft, fine muds and probably fed by ingesting the organic-rich sediments in which they lived.

The class Bivalvia (photos 172–207), as its name implies, is characterized by shells that are composed of two movable, interlocking valves separated by an elastic hinge composed of protein. Like the rostroconchs from which they evolved, early bivalves were at least partially buried in soft mud, most likely in areas of rapidly accumulating sediments rich in organic matter, or beneath waters rich in plankton. The increasingly complete enclosure of the animal by its shell resulted in a substantial decrease in mobility and thus an increased dependence on a stable food source.

The more primitive bivalves living today remain deposit feeders. However, the vast majority of bivalves extract food particles from seawater by pumping water across gills modified to serve as filters. This development of filter feeding resulted in an explosive proliferation of forms and has made the Bivalvia second only to Gastropoda in terms of diversity, both in number of species (about 8,000), and in variety of habitats. This early adaptation to a diet consisting of large volumes of microscopic particles resulted in the loss of the radula (rasping·teeth) in this class of mollusks. Surrounded by a shell, bivalves transferred sensory functions to those regions of the body having contact with the environment; the mantle edge, including siphons, and the foot. In time the head was lost.

The increasing success of the Bivalvia is believed to have contributed to the extinction of the presumably less well-adapted Rostroconchia.

The class Scaphopoda (plates 208–210) is the last to appear in the fossil record, and therefore is regarded as the last of the major molluscan groups to have evolved. Scaphopods produce single shells in the form of slightly curved, tusk-like, tapering tubes that are open at both ends. Anatomical and embryological evidence suggests that scaphopods are descended from rostroconchs, and that they preserve more of the primitive features of their extinct common ancestor than do bivalves.

Scaphopods live buried in sand or soft mud, with the narrow posterior end of the shell at or near the surface. They capture individual foraminiferans and other protozoans with the numerous thin tentacles called captacula that extend from either side of the animal's greatly reduced head. The microscopic, shelled prey is crushed by the radula, which is retained in these mollusks. The gills have been lost and respiration occurs through the walls of the mantle cavity. Scaphopods are a highly specialized and ecologically limited group of mollusks. According to recent estimates, there are about 350 living species.

Formation of the Molluscan Shell

All mollusks have a mantle. This specialized secretory region on the animal's upper surface produces a thin, flexible covering or cuticle composed of a specialized protein called conchiolin. The mantles of all mollusks also contain specialized cells that secrete a fluid from which the various forms of calcium carbonate can be crystallized.

In the most primitive mollusks, the Caudofoveata and Solenogastres, crystallization occurs within individual cells, which extrude long thin spines that penetrate and become embedded in the cuticle. In the other molluscan classes, fluid containing calcium carbonate is secreted into a confined region between the mantle and its protein covering. Crystallization occurs along the inner surface of the conchiolin, producing a continuously mineralized shell. The molluscan shell, a complex structure composed of mineral and organic components, forms outside of the animal's tissues.

The molluscan shell consists of multiple layers that vary in thickness, crystalline form and orientation (figure 7). Adjacent layers are often deposited with their crystal planes at right angles to each other, similar to the pattern seen in plywood. This greatly increases the strength of the shell. Most shells consist of three major components, each produced by a different region of the mantle (figure 8). The outermost protein layer, called the periostracum, is added along the edge of the shell by a specialized region of the adjacent mantle edge. An outer calcified layer is then laid down along the inner surface of the newly formed periostracum by a secretory region just within the mantle edge. An inner calcified layer, added along most of the remaining outer surface of the mantle, thickens and further strengthens the shell. An inevitable consequence of

(outside)

(inside)

FIGURE 7. An electron microscope photograph of the shell of *Busycon carica* (plate 117, left) broken parallel to the edge of the shell. Three different crystal layers can be seen.

this type of calcification, common to all shelled mollusks, is that growth can only occur by the addition of material to the shell edge. Once formed the shell cannot be modified, except for its internal layers. These consequences exert considerable limitations on the general architecture of the molluscan shell.

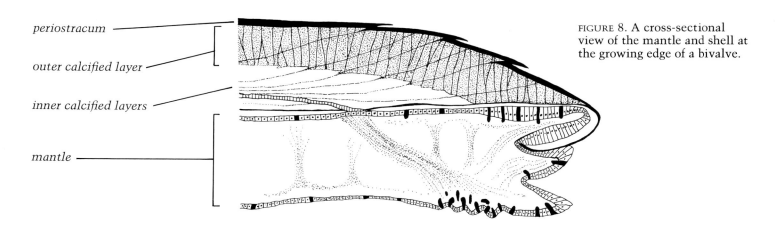

periostracum

outer calcified layer

inner calcified layers

mantle

FIGURE 8. A cross-sectional view of the mantle and shell at the growing edge of a bivalve.

16

The Coiled Shell: A Successful Experiment

Growth by addition of shell material to an existing edge will produce, in the most simple of circumstances, a conical shell. The shape of this cone, whether it is high or low, straight, curved or coiled, is affected by a variety of physical and environmental, as well as genetic factors.

A simple, low, cone-shaped shell of the type found in living monoplacophorans and the many groups of limpet-like gastropods is the most primitive of single shells. Increases in the height of the cone allowed for greater tissue volume as well as for more capacious mantle cavities, which in turn provided space for larger and more elaborate mantle cavity organs that were supported from the shell. However, an increase in shell height also raised the center of gravity of the animal, which made it increasingly unstable, especially on sand and mud bottoms. Some animals lowered their center of gravity by concentrating tissues at the base of the cone and sealing off the upper regions of the shells with partitions or septa. Others stabilized their increasingly taller shells by becoming at least partially buried in the sand. These solutions may have played respective roles in the origins of cephalopods and rostroconchs.

Coiling, however, is a far more ubiquitous method of lowering the center of gravity, as well as maintaining constant shell proportions. Examples of shells that conform to some portion of a logarithmic spiral can be found in all classes of single-shelled mollusks.

The number of theoretically possible types of coiled shell is infinite, yet the observed variety of forms is limited. It is evident to even the casual observer that many similar design themes are repeated in numerous, often unrelated groups of mollusks.

Anatomically symmetrical animals such as monoplacophorans, scaphopods and shelled cephalopods generally superimpose their bilateral symmetry onto their shells. This is accomplished through planispiral coiling (figure 9), that is, coiling in a single plane that corresponds to the plane of anatomical symmetry. Gastropods are anatomically asymmetrical animals. Their anatomical asymmetry is generally reflected in the helical coiling of their shell (figure 10). Bivalves are bilaterally symmetrical, and have shells composed of two valves, each a mirror image of the other. Each valve is helically coiled, and itself asymmetrical (figure 11).

A variety of environmental factors influence the architecture of the coiled molluscan shell. Among these are the availability of raw materials, the type of substrate, as

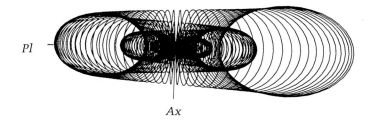

FIGURE 9. Computer simulation of a planispirally coiled shell similar to those of the nautiluses (plates 164–165). The axis of coiling (Ax) is perpendicular to the plane of symmetry (Pl).

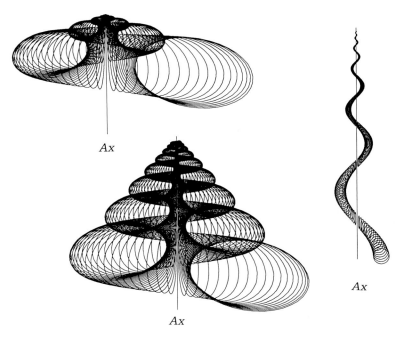

FIGURE 10. Computer simulation of three helically coiled gastropod shells, from left to right; *Gaza fisheri* (plate 19), *Maurea selecta* (plate 18) and an idealized vermetid similar to *Serpulorbis rousseaui* (plate 33). All the shells grow around an axis of coiling (Ax), but there is no longer a plane of shell symmetry.

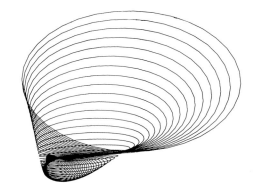

FIGURE 11. Computer simulation of one valve of the bivalve *Meiocardia moltkiana* (plate 198). Each valve mirrors the other, so that the plane of the page is the plane of symmetry for these bilaterally symmetrical animals.

well as the mollusk's requirements of protection, mobility and speed.

For example, although calcium is plentiful in tropical waters, its availability is limited in polar regions and the deep sea. Thus, shells tend to become thinner and more spherical towards the poles (plates 40, 83, 114) and with increasing depth (plates 17, 64, 186) in order to minimize the ratio of surface area to volume.

The type of bottom on which a mollusk lives greatly influences the shape of its shell. Mollusks that crawl along hard bottoms protect themselves from a variety of hazards by pulling their shells tightly against the substrate. These mollusks tend to have shells that are either limpet-like (plates 12, 16, 81, 104) or coiled cones (plates 11, 17, 21, 24). In such habitats the height of the shell generally does not exceed its diameter. In fact, it decreases with increasing exposure to such hazards as predators and wave action.

Mollusks living on the surface of sandy or rubble bottoms are faced with different requirements. Their shells may deviate from simple spiral geometry to produce either single, terminal (plates 47–53, 56–66) or periodic, regular (plates 70, 78, 84–102, 125, 132) expansions of the shell edge, generally for the purpose of stabilizing the shell in an aperture down orientation.

Mollusks living in calmer waters may produce shells with a wide variety of sculptural features, such as spines or webbing (plates 25–28, 89, 185, 187, 190). These features increase the effective volume of a shell well beyond that occupied by the animal. In addition to their more obvious antipredatory benefits, spines and webs also serve to increase the area on which other marine organisms can settle. These organisms may be important for their chemical as well as physical camouflage, since many predators detect their prey by the senses of smell and taste rather than by sight.

Mollusks that burrow in soft substrates place particular hydrodynamic requirements upon their shells. Many burrowing forms have elongated tapering shells (plates 35, 36, 74, 159, 208), often with smooth, rounded anterior ends to facilitate forward motion. The tapering posterior regions may have ribs or cords to minimize backward motion of the shell as the animal extends its foot forward through the sand, before again pulling the shell behind it. Many bivalves have elaborate surface sculpture that aids in burrowing, using a series of rocking motions (plates 189, 191). In several groups of burrowing gastropods, the shell is enveloped by the animal's tissues, and plays a less direct role in burrowing (plates 68, 69, 120–122, 161). Gastropods living on soft bottoms tend to be able to withdraw far enough into their shells to be beyond the reach of predators. Many are able to block their apertures with a hardened plug called an operculum.

Major deviations from coiling symmetry are generally associated with changes from a free living or mobile mode of life to one that is more stationary. For example, the larvae and free living juvenile snails of the genus *Serpulorbis* have regularly coiled shells. Once the animal permanently cements its shell to the substrate, shell growth becomes far less regular and coiling less evident (plate 33).

Most helically coiled shells are built upon the outer portions of preceding whorls, producing a solid shell axis (plates 36, 90, 127, 132) that adds to the strength of the shell. Coiled shells with a broad umbilicus or open space between opposing portions of whorls (plates 1, 34) are structurally weaker. Uncoiled shells (plates 32, 33, 37, 146) are weaker still. Most architectonicids (plate 34) and many epitoniids (plates 37, 38) are known to live in close association with corals or anemones, which may confer some supplemental protection against crushing predators.

These examples are but a small sampling of the interplay between environment and shell form.

BEYOND THE SHELL

Although a hard, calcified outer skeleton played a fundamental role in the evolution of the most successful molluscan classes, many of the more advanced members of several of these classes have greatly reduced shells or are shell-less. The initial advantages conferred by a shell, including protection from predators and environmental stresses, as well as support for tissues, allowed breakthroughs in functional thresholds, and resulted in a series of adaptive expansions into new habitats. Several groups of mollusks evolved alternative means of achieving these advantages. The shell, with its inherent constraints of weight and permanence of form, has been progressively reduced or eliminated in these animals. The transition from shelled to shell-less forms occurs in a series of stages. Several of these stages may be observed in remotely related groups of mollusks.

The first of these stages generally involves a reduction in the size and thickness of the shell. In the next stage the shell becomes internal, at first only when the animal is fully extended. Later the shell becomes greatly reduced and permanently internal. Once internal, the shell becomes decalcified during the course of evolution, and ultimately even the protein component of the shell may be lost.

Cephalopods are the most striking example of mollusks that have lost their shells. Over 98% of the species living today lack an external shell. Yet for these animals, the shell served as a buoyancy reservoir, as well as providing protection and support for tissues. The chambered nautiluses (plates 164–165) and the extinct ammonoids (plates 166–168) are examples of the early, shelled stages of cephalopod evolution.

In deep-sea squid of the genus *Spirula* (plate 169), the shell is internal, greatly reduced in size, yet calcified and spirally coiled. Its gas-filled chambers are separated by septa. Cuttlebone, the internal shell of cuttlefish, although chambered, is less densely calcified. In the squids, the shell has been further reduced, and is composed only of protein (plate 170). Most octopods have lost all vestiges of an internal shell.

The "shells" referred to as paper nautiluses (plate 171) are egg cases rather than true shells. Paper nautiluses are produced by female octopods of the genus *Argonauta* and are secreted by specialized tentacles, rather than at the mantle edge. The resemblance of these paper nautilus egg cases to the shells of nautiloids and ammonites is a testament to the functional constraints of environment on form.

These examples demonstrate how the various functions of the shell have been sequentially supplanted. Increased speed, maneuverability and camouflage protect the animal from predators. Once the heavy shell was abandoned, buoyancy was more easily regulated. The most recent function to be supplanted was tissue support, which occurred only in a relatively small number of bottom-dwelling cephalopods.

Several groups of prosobranch gastropods are in various stages of reducing the thickness of their shells, or developing internal shells. These include cowries (plates 56–65), naticids (plates 68, 69), and olives (plates 120–122). Within the class Gastropoda, the most striking diversifications of shell-less forms occur in the opisthobranchs. In this group, examples of all the stages can be observed, ranging from thick-shelled forms; through intermittently internal, thin-shelled forms (plate 161); permanently internal and decalcified shells; to the many totally shell-less groups such as the nudibranchs. In the nudibranchs, chemical defenses have obviated the need for shell. Many of these species feed on anemones and jellyfish, and some are able to transfer undischarged but functioning stinging cells (nematocysts) from their prey to their own skin for defensive purposes. Among the land snails, several groups have independently evolved into slugs.

Truly shell-less forms do not occur in the other molluscan classes, but there are species with reduced or internal shells in the Bivalvia and Polyplacophora. Bivalvia have specialized for burrowing in soft substrates. The shell thus assumed the additional function of defining a space into which increasingly voluminous gills could be suspended. Several bivalve groups developed the ability to burrow into substrates of increasing firmness, such as peat, wood and coral. In such substrates, the burrow walls defined the necessary volume. In some cases, the shells became greatly reduced, their primary purpose mechanical drilling. Several groups of bivalves have also evolved commensal or parasitic relationships with sea cucumbers or other marine invertebrates. Living within the body spaces of their hosts, these bivalves have greatly reduced, and often, internal shells. Among the eight-valved polyplacophorans, the acanthochitonid shell is enclosed by the mantle to varying degrees. In the Giant Pacific Chiton (*Cryptochiton stelleri*, plate 8), the shell plates are completely enclosed by the mantle.

It may seem bewildering that many of the most highly evolved descendants (slugs, nudibranchs, shipworms) of a group derived from a small, shell-less, worm-like ancestor would, after more than half a billion years, return to a relatively small, shell-less and worm-like condition. This merely underscores the fact that any form is but an interim solution to a particular problem of function, and is but a small indication of the plasticity and responsiveness of the molluscan form to the environment.

Mollusks have adapted, survived, and diversified far longer and far more successfully than most groups of organisms. Unlike most organisms, however, mollusks, especially shelled mollusks, have chronicled these progressive changes in the fossil record. Shells stand as monuments to the cumulative refinements of form by literally hundreds of millions of generations of mollusks. Their evolution offers an abundant source of material for recreation of the mind as well as of the eye.

M.G. Harasewych
Washington, D.C.

ACKNOWLEDGMENTS

Much of the impetus for this book was provided by the recent donation of the William D. Bledsoe collection of seashells to the National Museum of Natural History, Smithsonian Institution. As many of the truly exceptional and rare specimens figured in these pages are from this collection, I hope that in some small way this book may stand as a tribute to Mr. Bledsoe's passion for the beauty of shells.

Specimens for most of the remaining photographs were drawn from the collections of the National Museum of Natural History, Smithsonian Institution, which houses the largest and most extensive collection of mollusks in the world. I would also like to thank the following individuals for kindly making specimens available for photography: Donald Dan, Al and Beverly Deynzer, Lynn Funkhauser, Raye N. Germon, Leonard Hill, Robert and Dorothy Janowsky, Richard M. Kurz, Richard E. Petit, Edward J. Petuch, Peggy Williams, as well as several anonymous collectors.

Finally, I would like to express my appreciation to Nadia Mackiw for rendering the illustrations.

DIRECTED READINGS ON THE SUBJECT OF MOLLUSKS

INTRODUCTORY—GENERAL OVERVIEW

Abbott, R. T. *Kingdom of the Seashell.* New York: Crown Publishers, Inc., 1972. Well-illustrated overview of the biology of mollusks, as well as their uses by man.

Abbott, R. T. *Seashells of North America.* Revised Edition. New York: Golden Press, 1986. A well-illustrated identification guide to the common marine mollusks of North America.

Emerson, W. K. and Jacobson, M. K. *The American Museum Guide to Shells: Land, Freshwater, and Marine, from Nova Scotia to Florida.* New York: Alfred A. Knopf, 1976. A detailed identification guide to the land, freshwater and marine shell of the eastern United States.

Solem, G. A. *The Shell Makers, Introducing Mollusks.* New York: John Wiley & Sons, 1974. A good overview of the biology, ecology and evolution of mollusks. Particular emphasis is placed on land snails.

HISTORY

Dance, S. P. *A History of Shell Collecting.* Leiden: E. J. Brill, 1986. A well-documented and well-written history of man's use and study of shells.

Boss, Kenneth J. "Mollusca" ed. Parker, S.P. *Synopsis and Classification of Living Organisms.* New York: McGraw-Hill Book Company. Vol. 1, 1982. Provides a classification of the Mollusca from the level of phylum to families, includes short synopses of predominately anatomical diagnostic features. Technical.

Trueman, E. R. and Clarke, M.R. (eds.) "Evolution," *the Mollusca,* Vol. 10. New York: Academic Press, Inc. 1985.

Trueman, E. R. and Clarke, M. R. (eds.) "Form and Function," *The Mollusca,* Vol. 11, New York: Academic Press Inc., 1988.

Trueman, E. R. and Clarke, M. R. (eds.) "Paleontology and Neontology of Cephalopods," *The Mollusca,* Vol. 12. New York: Academic Press, Inc. 1988. Each contains a collection of articles on various aspects of the topic given by the volume title. Technical.

Yonge, C. M. and Thompson, T. E. *Living Marine Molluscs.* London: Collins. 1976. Excellent and readable general introduction into the biology of mollusks.

Pojeta, J., Runnegar, B., Peel, J.S., and Gordon, M. "Phylum Mollusca", *Fossil Invertebrates* eds. Boardman, R. S., Cheetham, A. H. and Rowell, A. J., Palo Alto: Blackwell Scientific Publications, 1987. Thorough overview of molluscan fossil record.

THE PLATES

CLASS
POLYPLACOPHORA

Family ISCHNOCHITONIDAE

Plate 5
Tonicella lineata (Wood, 1815)
LINED RED CHITON
North Pacific, Japan, Alaska to
San Diego, California
1 to 2 inches (2.5 to 5.0 cm)

Although brightly colored, this chiton is well camouflaged by the calcareous red algae upon which it lives and feeds.

Family MOPALIIDAE

Plate 6
Mopalia swanii Carpenter, 1864
SWAN'S CHITON
Alaska to Baja California
1 to 2 inches (2.5 to 5.0 cm)

Matching the coloration of the rocks and seaweeds on which it lives, this species is variable in color, ranging from green and brown to yellow and white. The head is situated at the lower end of the figured specimens.

Family CHITONIDAE

Plate 7
Chiton squamosus Linné, 1764
SQUAMOSE CHITON
West Indies and the Caribbean
2 to 3 inches (5.0 to 7.5 cm)

Like most chitons, these animals live on the underside of boulders during the day, and feed on algae primarily at night. Some species of chitons have radular teeth that contain iron, presumably to increase their durability.

Family ACANTHOCHITONIDAE

Plate 8
Cryptochiton stelleri (Middendorff, 1847)
GIANT PACIFIC CHITON
Japan, Alaska to Central California
6 to 14 inches (15 to 38 cm)

This species is by far the largest of the chitons. Larger specimens may be more than twenty years old. The shell, consisting of eight loosely fitted valves, is at least partially exposed in juvenile specimens, but becomes progressively enveloped by the girdle as the chitons grow. Unlike most chitons, this species may be found on sand below the low tide line.

PLATE 5

PLATE 6

PLATE 7

PLATE 8

CLASS
GASTROPODA

Family PLEUROTOMARIIDAE

Plate 9
Perotrochus midas F.M. Bayer, 1965
KING MIDAS'S SLIT SHELL
Bahamas and the northern Caribbean Sea
2 to 4 inches (5 to 10 cm)

Slit shells have long been regarded as the most primitive living snails because they retain paired mantle cavity organs such as gills, kidneys and certain glands. The rear of the slit, which separates the paired organs, is situated over the excretory and reproductive openings. The animal closes the forward portions of the slit with its mantle tissues, creating a tubular mantle cavity. Water enters the mantle cavity at the shell edge and exits at the rear of the slit, carrying excretory products. This species, the deepest dwelling slit shell (2,000 to 3,000 feet/600 to 900 meters), lives in perpetual darkness. Its iridescent golden orange shell would normally never be seen.

Plate 10
Perotrochus cf. *tangaroanus* Bouchet and Metivier, 1982
TANGAROA SLIT SHELL
New Zealand and northwestern Australia
3 to 4 inches (7.5 to 10 cm)

In this specimen, the outer calcareous layer has been dissolved with acid to reveal the iridescent, nacreous, inner calcareous layer.

Plate 11
Entemnotrochus adansonianus (Fischer and Crosse), 1861
ADANSON'S SLIT SHELL
Western Atlantic Ocean from Bermuda to Brazil
4 to 8 inches (10 to 20 cm)

This group of slit shells, characterized by a very long slit (indicative of a deep mantle cavity) and an open shell axis, occurs in shallower waters (260 to 820 feet/80 to 250 meters) that are penetrated by light. This specimen was collected while feeding on an intensely yellow sponge, suggesting that its yellowish coloration may be due to unmetabolized sponge pigments. Red and white specimens such as the one in plates 1 and 2 were collected feeding on a white sponge that contained red algae.

Family HALIOTIDAE

Plate 12
Haliotis asinina Linné, 1758
DONKEY'S EAR ABALONE
Southwestern Pacific Ocean
2 to 4 inches (5 to 10 cm)

and *Haliotis elegans* Philippi, 1874
ELEGANT ABALONE
Western Australia
2 to 3 inches (5 to 7 cm)

Like slit shells, abalones have paired mantle cavity organs. Instead of a slit, this group of snails has a series of round holes. As the shell grows, new holes are added at the shell edge, while the oldest holes are sealed over with shell material.

Plates 13/14
Haliotis scalaris Leach, 1814
STAIRCASE ABALONE
Southern and Western Australia
2 to 5 inches (5 to 12.5 cm)

Like many snails that live on hard bottoms, abalones have evolved a limpetlike shell. Unlike limpets, abalones continue to coil, but become flattened by canting the plane of the aperture until it is nearly perpendicular to the axis of coiling. This axis is clearly visible in the photographs.

Family FISSURELLIDAE

Plate 15
Fissurella barbadensis (Gmelin, 1791)
BARBADOS KEYHOLE LIMPET
Florida to Brazil
1 to 1.5 inches (2.5 to 4 cm)

The shells of the free-swimming limpet larvae are helically coiled, but become bilaterally symmetrical after the larvae settle. The keyhole limpets retain paired mantle cavity organs. Water enters the mantle cavity along the forward edges of the shell, and exits volcano-like through the single, keyhole-shaped aperture at the top of the shell.

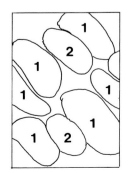

Plate 12
1. *Haliotis asinina*
2. *Haliotis elegans*

Family PATELLIDAE

Plate 16
Patella longicosta Lamarck, 1819
LONG-RIBBED LIMPET
Southern Africa
2 to 2.5 inches (5 to 6 cm)

Patella oculus Born, 1778
SOUTH AFRICAN EYE LIMPET
Southwestern Africa
3 to 4 inches (7.5 to 10 cm)

Patella granatina Linné, 1758
SANDPAPER LIMPET
Southern Africa
2 to 3 inches (5 to 7.5 cm)

Cellana grata (Gould, 1859)
JAPANESE GRATA LIMPET
Japan and Korea
1 to 2 inches (2.5 to 5 cm)

Patella miniata Born, 1778
CINNABAR LIMPET
Southern Africa
1 to 2 inches (2.5 to 5 cm)

The limpet shell form has arisen many times in the course of gastropod evolution. It is generally indicative of animals that live on hard bottoms and feed on algae or encrusting organisms. Even this basic shell form varies in response to environmental factors. Limpets become flatter with increasing wave energy and with increased abundance of crushing predators such as crabs. The radial ridges and troughs of the Long-Ribbed Limpet, for example, not only buttress the shell, adding to its strength, but also redirect and channel the force of the breaking waves. Similar features can be observed in barnacles that live in the same habitat.

These and all subsequent snails have only one compliment of the primitively paired mantle cavity organs. These are situated on the left side of the mantle cavity. The excretory and reproductive openings have been moved forward along the right side of the mantle cavity. Water enters the mantle cavity along the animal's left side, passes over the gill, purges the rear of the mantle cavity and exits after passing over the excretory and reproductive openings along the right side of the mantle cavity.

Family TROCHIDAE

Plate 17
Calliostoma atlantis Clench and Aguayo, 1940
ATLANTIS TOP SHELL
Off Cuba and the Bahamas
1 to 1.5 inches (2.5 to 4 cm)

This specimen, only the second known, was collected at a depth of 3,000 feet (900 meters). Although the shell lacks pigment, the animal is bright red.

Plate 18
Maurea selecta (Dillwyn, 1817)
SELECT MAUREA
New Zealand
1 to 2.5 inches (2.5 to 6 cm)

This variable species lives on sandy bottoms from below the tide line to depths of about 300 feet (90 meters). Specimens from deeper water tend to be larger and taller, and to have paler coloration.

Plate 19
Gaza fischeri Dall, 1889
FISCHER'S GAZA
Greater and Lesser Antilles
1 to 1.5 inches (2.5 to 4 cm)

Gazas live on soft bottoms at depths in excess of 2,500 feet (750 meters). When disturbed, specimens have been observed to swim by undulating their large, broad foot.

Plate 20
Clanculus pharaonius (Linné, 1758)
MANTLE CLANCULUS
Indian Ocean
0.5 to 0.8 inch (1 to 2 cm)

This species tends to live in fairly dense populations on the undersides of rocky rubble that is exposed at low tide. There is little variation in coloration or shape among individual specimens, suggesting a uniform habitat.

Plate 21
Tegula regina Stearns, 1892
QUEEN TEGULA
Central California, western coast of Baja Peninsula
1 to 2 inches (2.5 to 5 cm)

This uncommon species lives at depths of 20 to 100 feet (6 to 30 meters) on rocky rubble bottoms.

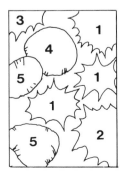

Plate 16
1. *Patella longicosta*
2. *Patella oculus*
3. *Patella granatina*
4. *Cellans grata*
5. *Patella miniata*

Family STOMATELLIDAE

Plate 22
Stomatella planulata Lamarck, 1816
FLATTENED STOMATELLA
Southwestern Pacific Ocean
1 to 1.5 inches (2.5 to 4 cm)

Only remotely related to the abalones, these animals live in a similar habitat. The shells of stomatellas and abalones converge on the flattened, limpet-like form in a similar fashion.

Family TURBINIIDAE

Plate 23
Turbo reevei Philippi, 1847
REEVE'S TURBAN
Central Western Pacific
1.5 to 2.5 inches (3 to 6 cm)

This extremely variable species is a common denizen of shallow reefs. Unlike most turbinids, its exterior is glossy and free of encrusting organisms.

Plate 24
Turbo sarmaticus Linné, 1758
SOUTH AFRICAN TURBAN
South Africa
2 to 4 inches (4 to 10 cm)

Although large specimens are often dull, encrusted or abraded, juveniles (lower right) exhibit elaborate, banded color patterns. This species is common on rocky bottoms below the low tide line.

Plate 25
Guildfordia yoka Jousseaume, 1888
YOKA STAR TURBAN
Japan
2 to 3 inches (5 to 7 cm)

Star turbans, which live in deep (300 to 1,500 feet/100 to 500 meters), calm waters, periodically add long spines perpendicular to their shell margin. These not only increase the effective size of the shell, but make it more difficult for a potential predator to turn the shell over and expose the aperture.

Plate 26
Astraea heliotropium (Martyn, 1784)
SUNBURST STAR TURBAN
New Zealand
3 to 4 inches (7 to 10 cm)

Restricted to the deeper waters of the Cook's Strait, this species was first brought up on one of the cables of the H.M.S. *Adventure*, Captain Cook's ship.

Plate 27
Bolma girgyllus (Reeve, 1861)
GIRGYLLUS STAR SHELL
Philippines
2 inches (5 cm)

This species lives at depths of several hundred feet, and is extremely variable in coloration and degree of spine development.

Plate 28
Angaria sphaerula (Kiener, 1839)
[*lower left*]
KIENER'S DELPHINULA
Philippines

and *Angaria vicdani* Kosuge, 1980
[*top & lower right*]
DAN'S DELPHINULA
Philippines
Both 2 to 3 inches (5 to 7 cm) including spines

The intricate and extremely delicate spines of these deep-water species are usually heavily overgrown with corals and other invertebrates. It takes many hours of painstaking cleaning to reveal the true beauty of these shells.

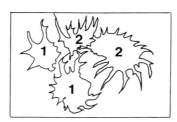

Plate 28
1. *Anagaria sphaerula* 2. *Angaria vicdani*

Family NERITIDAE

Plate 29
Nerita peloronta Linné, 1758
BLEEDING TOOTH NERITE
Tropical Western Atlantic
1 to 1.5 inches (2.5 to 3.5 cm)

The tropical family Neritidae contains species that have successfully adapted to life in fresh water. Marine species such as the Bleeding Tooth Nerite are generally restricted to wave-beaten rocks exposed at low tide. Others can be found in muddy brackish estuaries or in mangrove swamps.

Family LITTORINIDAE

Plate 30
Littorina zebra Donovan, 1825
[*three specimens*]
ZEBRA PERIWINKLE
West Coast Central America
1 to 1.5 inches (2.5 to 3.5 cm)

and *Tectarius pagodus* (Linné, 1758)
[*one specimen*]
PAGODA PRICKLY-WINKLE
Southwestern Pacific
1 to 2 inches (2.5 to 5 cm)

Like nerites, periwinkles inhabit tropical and semitropical rocky shores. *Littorina zebra* live on seaweed-covered rocks in the zone between the low and high tide lines. Species of *Tectarius* often live 3 feet or more above the high tide line, relying on wave spray for moisture. Their chalky white shells match the color and texture of the sun-baked limestone on which they live.

PLATE 9

PLATE 10

PLATE 11

PLATE 12

PLATE 13

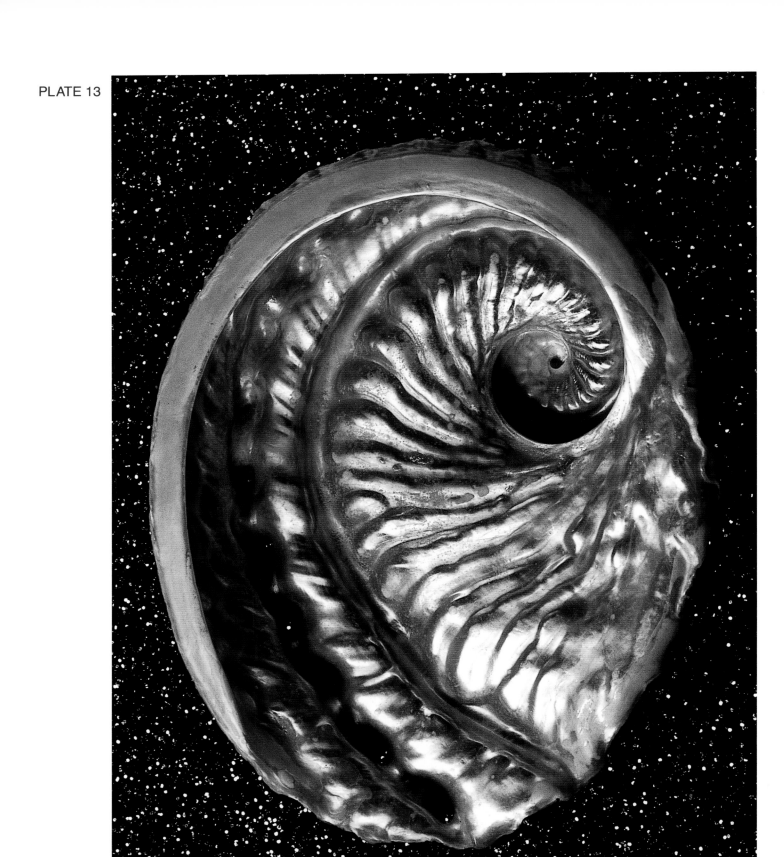

PLATE 14

PLATE 15

PLATE 16

PLATE 17

PLATE 18

PLATE 19

PLATE 20

PLATE 21

PLATE 22

PLATE 23

PLATE 24

41

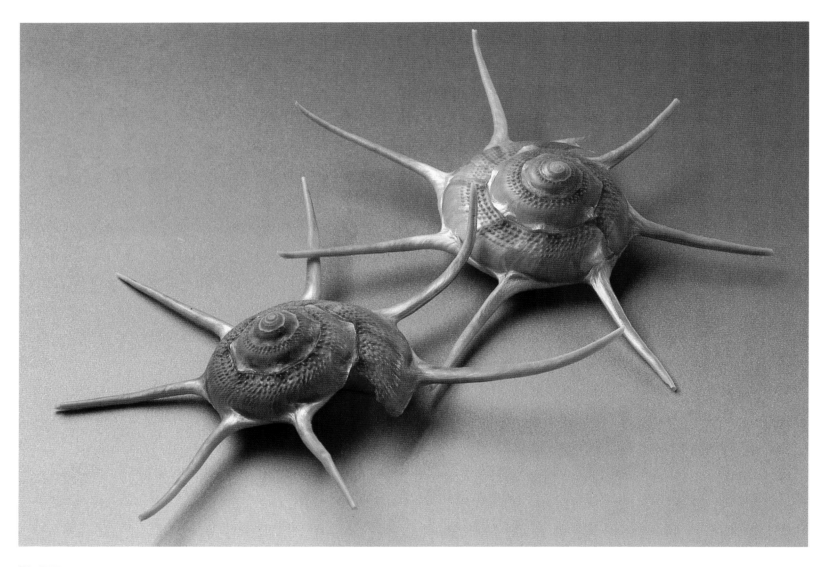

PLATE 25

PLATE 26

PLATE 27

PLATE 28

PLATE 29

PLATE 30

Family TURRITELLIDAE

Plate 31
Turritella terebra (Linné, 1758)
SCREW TURRITELLA
Southwestern Pacific
2 to 6 inches (5 to 15 cm)

Long, narrow conical shells are indicative of snails that live on, or burrow in, sand or soft mud. Turritellas occur in dense beds on sand and mud bottoms below the low tide line. These animals remain buried just below the surface and feed by filtering suspended matter from the water with their gills, much like bivalves.

Family SILIQUARIIDAE

Plate 32
Siliquaria squamata Blainville, 1827
SLIT WORM-SHELL
Tropical Western Atlantic
1 to 3 inches (2.5 to 7.5 cm)

Species in the family Siliquariidae live embedded in the walls of living sponges. Like turritellids, they feed by filtering microorganisms from the seawater. Immobile and encased in sponge tissue, many of the functional constraints on shell geometry are relaxed. Growth must keep pace with the sponge in order to maintain the shell aperture at or above the surface of the sponge.

Family VERMETIDAE

Plate 33
Serpulorbis rousseaui (Vaillant, 1871)
ROUSSEAU'S WORM SHELL
Western Pacific Ocean
Individual shells 2 to 6 inches in length (5 to 15 cm)

Free crawling juvenile vermetids resemble miniature turritellas. After the juvenile shell is cemented to a hard substrate like the soft coral in the figured example, growth becomes progressively more irregular, and is directed away from the substrate. Vermetids secrete sticky sheets of mucus to which planktonic organisms adhere. These sheets are periodically drawn in and swallowed. Neighboring animals tend to grow away from each other, in order to avoid entangling their mucus nets.

Family ARCHITECTONICIDAE

Plate 34
Architectonica perspectiva (Linné, 1758)
CLEAR SUNDIAL
Indian and Pacific Oceans
1 to 2 inches (2.5 to 5 cm)

Most members of this family are associated with cnidarians, especially hard and soft corals. This species tends to be locally common on sandy bottoms at depths of 20 or more feet.

Family POTAMIDIDAE

Plate 35
Telescopium telescopium (Linné, 1758)
TELESCOPE SNAIL
Indian and Pacific Ocean
3 to 4 inches (7 to 10 cm)

These amphibious animals inhabit muddy bottoms in mangrove swamps. They do not burrow, but drag their ponderous shells behind them as they plow through the soft mud, feeding on silt and detritus.

Family CAMPANILIDAE

Plate 36
Campanile symbolicum Iredale, 1917
[center]
BELL CLAPPER
Western Australia
5 to 8 inches (12 to 20 cm)

Family CERITHIIDAE

Pseudovertagus phylarchus (Iredale, 1929)
AMULET VERTAGUS *[left]*
Southwestern Pacific Ocean
2 to 3 inches (5 to 8 cm)

and *Cerithioclava garciai* Houbrick, 1986
GARCIA'S CERITH
Honduras
[right]
2 to 4 inches (5 to 10 cm)

As can be surmised from their elongate, conical shells, these few representatives of a major group of snails, the ceriths, all inhabit soft bottoms. *Campanile* lives on a rubble bottom, and does not burrow, its shell often overgrown with algae. The other species are more usual in that they live on fine, clean sand, and burrow at least partially. All clearly show the position of the inhalent siphon at the anterior of the shell. A posterior, exhalent channel is visible along the side of *Cerithioclava garciai*.

Family EPITONIIDAE

Plate 37
Epitonium scalare (Linné, 1758)
PRECIOUS WENTLETRAP
Western Pacific Ocean
1 to 2 inches (2.5 to 5 cm)

The wentletraps are snails that have evolved a highly specialized diet. All species studied to date feed on coelenterates. Some forage for sea anemones and totally devour small individuals. Others live in close association with larger anemones or solitary corals, feeding repeatedly on their tissues. After feeding, these wentletraps burrow near the anemone's base, relying on it for defense against predators. The delicate shell of the Precious Wentletrap may be an indication of dependence on protection by a coelenterate host.

Although these shells may wash up in parts of Australia by the thousands after a storm, this shell was one of the great treasures of the collections of the 18th century. In 1767, a single specimen was auctioned for 900 francs, while a painting by El Greco sold at the same auction for 24 francs.

Plate 38
Sthenorytis pernobilis (Fischer and Bernardi, 1857)
NOBLE WENTLETRAP [*bottom*]
Carolinas to Lesser Antilles
1 to 2 inches (2.5 to 5 cm)

and *Amaea magnifica* (Sowerby, 1844)
MAGNIFICENT WENTLETRAP
[*top*]
Western Pacific Ocean
2 to 3 inches (5 to 7 cm)

The thick shell and broad, well-buttressed webs would make burrowing difficult for the Noble Wentletrap. Limited observations indicate that this species may forage for smaller anemones on rocky bottoms in 650 feet (200 meters) of water. Nothing is known of the biology of the Magnificent Wentletrap, which lives in comparable depths.

Family JANTHINIDAE

Plate 39
Janthina janthina (Linné, 1758)
COMMON JANTHINA
Worldwide, Tropical Seas
1 to 2 inches (2.5 to 5 cm)

These gregarious snails float at the sea surface on "bubble rafts" composed of mucus and air, where they feed on floating jellyfish such as the Portuguese-Man-of War. Their shells are thin, to minimize weight. These two-toned shells are an example of protective coun-

tershading. The animal floats with the darker surface uppermost. When viewed from above, the shell blends with the deep blue of the open sea. When viewed from below, the lighter lower surface blends with the color of the sky. Countershading is a defense against predators that hunt by sight, such as birds and fish.

Family TRICHOTROPIDAE

Plate 40
Torellia mirabilis E.A. Smith, 1907
MARVELOUS TORELLIA
Antarctica
1 to 2 inches (2.5 to 5 cm)

The shell of this snail, which lives at depths of over 600 feet (180 meters), is composed almost entirely of periostracum, the outermost protein layer of the shell. It contains so little calcium carbonate as to be compressible to the touch.

Family CREPIDULIDAE

Plate 41
Crucibulum scutellatum (Wood, 1828)
SHIELD CUP-AND-SAUCER SHELL
Baja California to Ecuador

Members of this family of filter-feeding snails have independently evolved the limpet-like form. As these animals live in regions with predominantly sandy or muddy shores, their free-swimming larvae, which have coiled shells, do not metamorphose until they find suitable hard substrates, such as horseshoe crabs or the shells of other mollusks, on which to settle. The inner conical structure supports the fragile liver and gonads.

Plate 42
Crepidula plana Say, 1822
WHITE SLIPPER SHELL
Eastern North America
1 to 1.5 inches (2 to 3 cm)

Shells of this species attach to the inner surfaces of large, empty shells, and conform to their concave surfaces.

Family XENOPHORIDAE

Plate 43/44
Xenophora conchyliophora (Born, 1780)
ATLANTIC CARRIER SHELL
Carolinas to Brazil
1 to 2.5 inches (2.5 to 6 cm)

The carrier shells are best known for their ability to attach foreign material such as stones, shells and pieces of coral onto the upper surfaces of their own shells. These snails live on sand and rubble bottoms, feeding on organic matter and foraminiferans collected from the substrate beneath the rim of their shell. They move by extending their foot to raise the shell, then falling forward.

Plate 45
Stellaria solaris (Linné, 1767)
SUNBURST CARRIER SHELL
Indian and Pacific Oceans
3 to 4 inches (7 to 10 cm)

Like the Atlantic Carrier Shell, the Sunburst Carrier Shell cements objects to its shell when young. As the shell grows larger, periodic tubular spines are produced at its margin and objects are no longer cemented to its surface. Like stilts, these spines raise the shell off the sea floor.

Plate 46
Tugurium longleyi (Bartsch, 1931)
LONGLEY'S CARRIER SHELL [*upper*]
Carolinas to Barbados
3 to 5 inches (7.5 to 12.5 cm)

and *Onustus exustum* (Reeve, 1843)
BARREN CARRIER SHELL [*lower*]
Indian and Western Pacific Oceans
2 to 3 inches (5 to 7.5 cm)

Both these species produce broad flanges or skirts along their margins that serve to raise the base of the shell above the surface of the ocean bottom. Neither cement foreign material onto their shell beyond the juvenile stages. At least in the case of *Tugurium longleyi*, this is due to the fact that the animal lives on bottoms composed of fine sediments on which larger objects are rarely encountered.

Family APORRHAIDAE

Plate 47

Aporrhais occidentalis Beck, 1836
AMERICAN PELICAN'S FOOT
Western North Atlantic Ocean

Aporrhais pesgallinae Barnard, 1963
AFRICAN PELICAN'S FOOT
Southwestern African Coast

and *Aporrhais pespelecani* Linné, 1758
COMMON PELICAN'S FOOT
Eastern North Atlantic

All range from 1 to 2 inches (2.5 to 5 cm)

Upon reaching adult size, animals of the genus *Aporrhais* produce a thick, broad flaring extension of their outer shell edge. This serves to stabilize the shell in an aperture down orientation. As these animals burrow in sand or mud bottoms, their flared shell edge forms the ceiling of a feeding compartment complete with openings for inhalent and exhalent currents. Patterns of digitations on this flared extension are used to distinguish the various species, and are indicative of the texture of the substrate for which individual species are adapted.

Family STROMBIDAE

Plate 48/49

Strombus gallus Linné, 1758
ROOSTER-TAIL CONCH
Tropical Atlantic, Florida to Brazil
4 to 5 inches (10 to 12.4 cm)

Conchs are relatively large herbivorous snails that live on the surface of sand and rubble bottoms in tropical seas. Encumbered by thick, heavy shells, these animals have a distinctive manner of locomotion. The animal extends itself as far forward as possible, anchors its foot with the aid of its operculum, then raises itself and lurches its shell forward. The elongated extensions of the flared shell edge extend over the foot in its forwardmost, as well as rearmost, positions.

Plate 47
1. *Aporrhais occidentalis*
2. *Aporrhais pesgallinae*
3. *Aporrahis pespelicani*

Plate 50

Strombus listeri T. Gray, 1852
LISTER'S CONCH
Northern Indian Ocean
4 to 6 inches (10 to 15 cm)

This thin-shelled conch lives at depths of 160 to 330 feet (50 to 100 meters). It may be the deepest dwelling member of the family.

Plate 51

Strombus sinuatus Lightfoot, 1786
LACINIATE CONCH
Southwestern Pacific
3.5 to 5 inches (8 to 12.5 cm)

Once the flaring outer lip is produced, the shell ceases to grow, although it generally becomes thicker and heavier with age. Energy formerly used for growth is devoted to reproduction.

Plate 52

Lambis violacea (Swainson, 1821)
VIOLET SPIDER CONCH
Western Indian Ocean
3 to 4 inches (7.5 to 10 cm)

Spider conchs are restricted in their distribution to the Indian and Pacific Oceans. Like *Strombus*, to which they are closely related, these animals feed on filamentous algae.

Plate 53

Lambis truncata sebae (Kiener, 1843)
SEBA'S SPIDER CONCH
Red Sea and tropical Pacific Ocean
10 to 12 inches (25 to 30 cm)

The largest of the spider conchs, this species lives on sandy patches near coral reefs, generally at depths of 15 to 40 feet (5 to 10 meters).

Plate 54

Tibia powisi (Petit, 1842)
POWIS'S TIBIA
Southwestern Pacific
2 to 2.5 inches (5 to 6 cm)

All members of the genus *Tibia* are characterized by a long, narrow extension of the shell aperture that encases the siphon, a tubular region of the mantle edge that directs inhalant water currents. These herbivorous animals live on soft, muddy bottoms in deep water. The siphonal canal may support the siphon above the mud and protect it from grazing by fish and crabs while the animals are buried.

Plate 55

Terebellum terebellum (Linné, 1758)
TEREBELLUM CONCH
Indian and Pacific Oceans
2 to 3 inches (5 to 7 cm)

Unlike most members of the family Strombidae, the Terebellum Conch is a rapid and effective burrower. This is reflected in its streamlined shell.

PLATE 31

PLATE 32

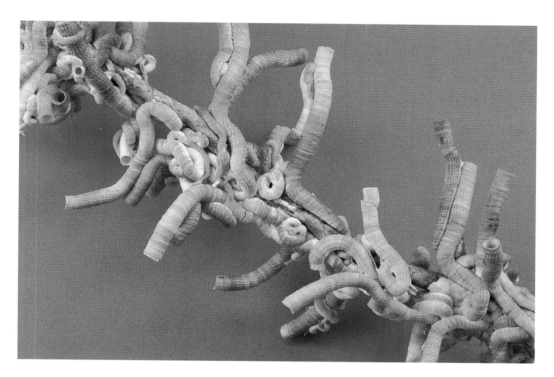

PLATE 33

PLATE 34

54

PLATE 35

PLATE 36

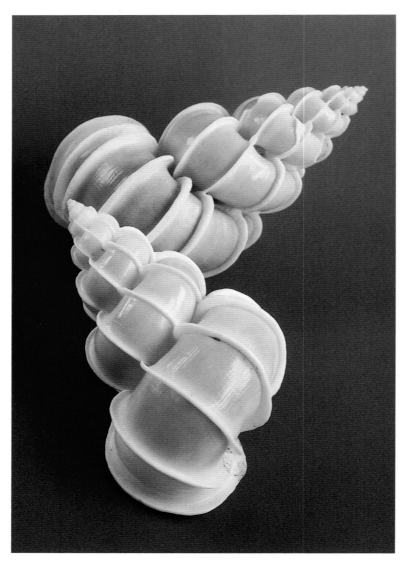

PLATE 37

PLATE 38

PLATE 39

PLATE 40

PLATE 41

PLATE 42

PLATE 43

PLATE 44

PLATE 45

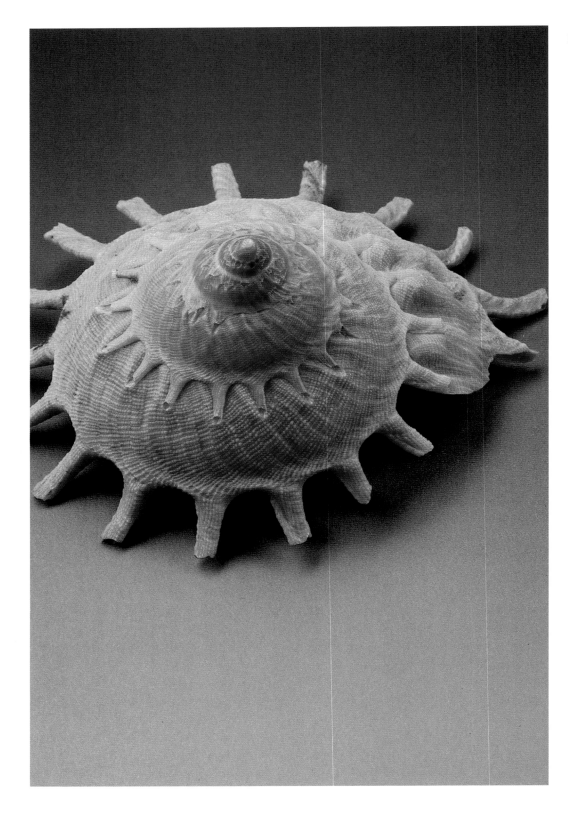

PLATE 46

PLATE 47

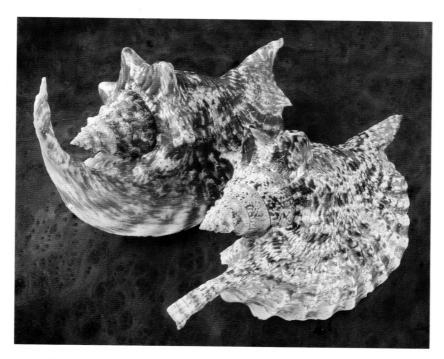

PLATE 48

PLATE 49

PLATE 50

PLATE 51

PLATE 52

PLATE 53

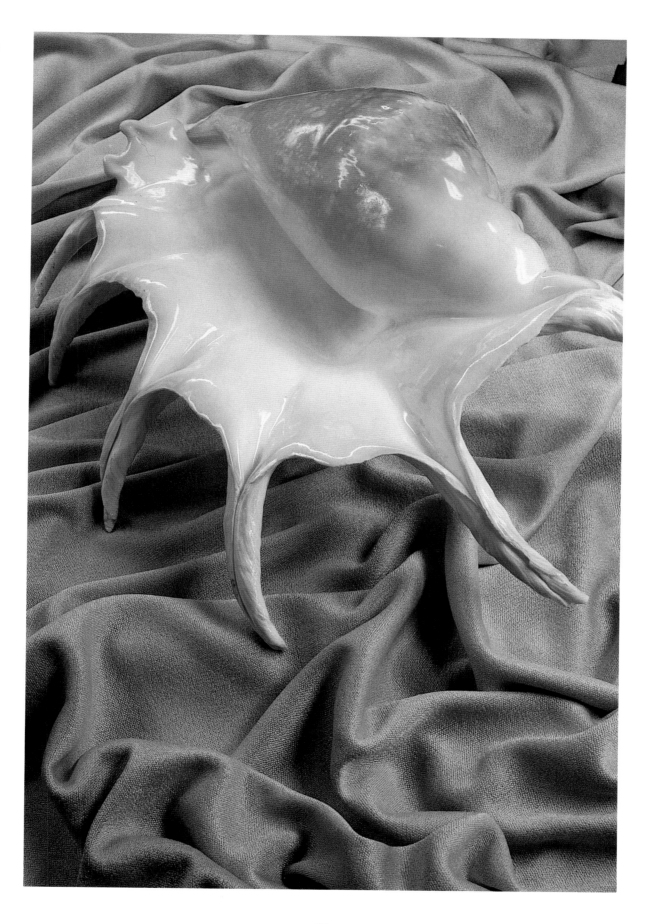

PLATE 54

PLATE 55

Family CYPRAEIDAE

Plate 56
Cypraea ziczac Linné, 1758
ZIGZAG COWRIE
Indian and Pacific Oceans
0.8 inch (2 cm)

Like most snails, cowries begin life with typical, helically coiled shells. The final whorl, however, becomes greatly expanded and envelops all preceding whorls. The edges of the mantle envelop the entire shell, producing its glossy surface. Juvenile cowries are uniformly colored or simply banded. The characteristic color patterns of the adult shell are deposited in a series of layers.

Plate 57
Cypraea guttata Gmelin, 1791
GREAT SPOTTED COWRIE
Western Pacific and northeastern Indian Oceans
1.5 to 3 inches (4 to 7.5 cm)

Adult cowrie shells appear nearly bilaterally symmetrical, with the aperture oriented from front to back. Water enters through a short siphon at the more tapered forward end and leaves at the rear. Although the shell of this deep water cowry is brightly colored, the mantle that covers it in life is mottled brown and tan with many long, branching tendrils or papillae on its outer surface. The colorful raised ribs on the base of the shell may act to guide the mantle while it is being retracted or extended.

Plate 58
Cypraea cribraria Linné, 1758
SIEVE COWRIE
Indian and Pacific Oceans
1 inch (2.5 cm)

This species lives under rocks and coral rubble in shallow water. It is more active at night. The shell is narrow and streamlined, making passage through narrow crevices easier. The mantle is bright red, the papillae short and blunt.

Plate 59/60
Cypraea leucodon Broderip, 1828
[plate 59, aperture view;
plate 60, bottom]
WHITE-TOOTHED COWRIE
Philippines, Maldives and Solomons
3 to 4 inches (7.5 to 10 cm)

and *Cypraea valentia* Perry, 1811
[plate 60, top]
PRINCE COWRIE
Philippines to Fiji
2.5 to 4 inches (6.2 to 10 cm)

Both of these species were, until recently, of legendary rarity. Both live in deep water, under ledges and in caves along the outer edges of coral reefs. The mantle of the Prince Cowrie is thin and nearly transparent, with long, highly branched papillae.

Plate 61
Cypraea caurica Linné, 1758
CAURICA COWRIE
Indian and Pacific Oeans
1.5 inches (4 cm)

and *Cypraea eglantina* Duclos, 1833
EGLANTINE COWRIE
Central Pacific Ocean
2.5 inches (6 cm)

Both of these species are common throughout their broad geographic ranges. In a small region along the southern coast of New Caledonia however, these as well as many other species of cowries develop a characteristic dark brown overglaze. The occurrence of similar coloration in a wide variety of species suggests that this phenomenon is due to local environmental conditions.

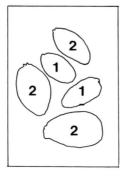

Plate 61
1. *Cypraea caurica*
2. *Cypraea eglantina*

Plate 62
Cypraea tessellata Swainson, 1822
[large and small right]
CHECKERBOARD COWRIE
Endemic to Hawaii
0.8 to 2 inches (2 to 5 cm)

and *Cypraea porteri* C. Cate, 1966
[large left]
PORTER'S COWRIE
Philippines and Central Pacific Ocean
1.5 to 2.5 inches (4 to 6 cm)

The Checkerboard Cowrie is restricted to the Hawaiian Islands, where it lives under dead coral slabs and in crevices in the reef. The smaller size is the more usual. The closely related Porter's Cowrie is far more rare, despite its broader geographic range.

Plate 63
Zoila rosselli (Cotton, 1948)
ROSSELL'S COWRIE
Western Australia
2 to 3 inches (5 to 7.5 cm)

Like all other members of the genus *Zoila*, Rossell's Cowrie has been reported to feed selectively on sponges at depths ranging from 16 to 230 feet (5 to 70 meters). The smooth mantle is blackish-brown, like the shell. Some specimens have a lighter patch or streak on their backs, indicating the limits to which the mantle was extended.

Plate 64
Cypraea cruikshanki Kilburn, 1972
CRUIKSHANK'S COWRIE
South Africa
1 inch (2.5 cm)

This thin-shelled, nearly spherical cowrie occurs at depths ranging from about 1,300 to 2,300 feet (400 to 700 meters). It is the deepest dwelling species of cowrie presently known.

Family OVULIDAE

Plate 65
Jenneria pustulata (Lightfoot, 1786)
JENNER'S COWRIE
Sea of Cortez to Ecuador
0.8 inches (2 cm)

Like many cowries and most ovulids, this species feeds on soft corals. Coloration and texture of shell and mantle blend with the encrusted rocks on which these animals live.

Plate 66
Volva volva (Linné, 1758)
SHUTTLECOCK VOLVA
Indian and Pacific Oceans
3 to 4 inches (7.5 to 10 cm)

The long canals of this distinct species serve to maximize the distance between inhalant and exhalant currents.

Plate 67
Phenacovolva rosea nectarea Iredale, 1930
SWEET OVULID
Eastern Australia
1 inch (2.5 cm)

Like most ovulids, this species lives on soft corals or sea fans. The animals and their shells closely match the color of the host coral, probably because they incorporate pigment from the tissues upon which they feed.

Family NATICIDAE

Plate 68
Natica turtoni E.A. Smith, 1890
[*banded*]
TURTON'S MOON SHELL
Western Africa
1.5 inches (4 cm)

Natica stellata Chenu, 1845
[*orange mottled*]
STARRY MOON SHELL
Western Pacific Ocean
1.5 inches (4 cm)

Neverita sagamiensis (Pilsbry, 1904)
[*brown & white*]
SAGAMI BAY MOON SHELL
Japan
1.5 inch (4 cm)

Polinices tumidus (Swainson, 1840)
[*remaining three*]
PEAR-SHAPED MOON SHELL
Indian and Pacific Oceans
1.5 inch (4 cm)

Although not obvious from the nearly spherical shapes of their shells, moon snails burrow rapidly and effectively through sand and mud. The animal inflates its tissues with seawater until its volume far exceeds the volume of the shell. These tissues envelop the shell almost completely and give the animal an overall wedge-shaped appearance.

Plate 69
Sinum perspectivum (Say, 1831)
BABY'S EAR MOON
Carolinas to the West Indies
1 to 2 inches (2.5 to 5 cm)

In this group of moon snails the shell has become flattened and reduced in size. Although it resembles the shell of abalones in general shape, it is far too small to cover the animal.

Family CASSIDAE

Plate 70
Phalium granulatum (Born, 1778)
[*larger*]
SCOTCH BONNET
Carolinas to Brazil
2 to 3 inches (5 to 7.5 cm)

and *Phalium labiatum iheringi* (Carcelles, 1953)
[*smaller*]
IHERING'S BONNET
Brazil to Argentina
1 to 2 inches (2.5 to 5 cm)

The lack of encrusting organisms on the back of the shells indicates that these animals spend considerable time completely buried in the sand. These rapidly

burrowing snails are voracious predators of sand dollars and sea urchins.

Family FICIDAE

Plate 71
Ficus ventricosa (Sowerby, 1825)
[*top*]
SWOLLEN FIG SHELL
West coast of Mexico to Peru
3 to 4 inches (7.5 to 10 cm)

and *Ficus gracilis* (Sowerby, 1825)
[*two bottom*]
GRACEFUL FIG SHELL
Eastern Asia
4 to 5 inches (10 to 12.5 cm)

These predatory snails live on sandy bottoms below tide levels where they feed on echinoderms such as sand dollars. The streamlined shell, broad foot and lack of an operculum are all indicative of predatory snails that burrow in the sand.

Family TONNIDAE

Plate 72
Malea ringens (Swainson, 1822)
GRINNING TUN
West coast of Mexico to Peru
6 to 7 inches (15 to 17.5 cm)

Among the tun shells, this species is unusual in having a thickened apertural edge or lip buttressed with denticles. Reinforcement of the outer shell edge is a common defense against predation by crabs that break or peel back the shell edge with their claws, until they expose the retracted snail.

Plate 73
Tonna galea (Linné, 1758)
GIANT TUN
Worldwide Tropics
6 to 8 inches (15 to 20 cm)

Although thin-shelled, tuns are extremely aggressive. Their salivary glands produce sulfuric acid with which tuns dissolve holes in the shells of sea urchins on which they feed. The larvae of most tuns spend weeks to months floating in the plankton before settling to the bottom. This results in extremely broad geographic ranges.

Family RANELLIDAE

Plate 74
Charonia tritonis (Linné, 1758)
TRUMPET TRITON
Tropical Indian and Pacific Oceans
12 to 18 inches (30 to 45 cm)

This large colorful animal is a voracious predator, roaming coral reefs for starfish and other echinoderms. Although the streamlined shell is well suited for burrowing, this animal hunts on the surface of the sand and only partially buries itself when inactive.

Plate 75
Cymatium parthenopeum (von Salis, 1793)
GIANT HAIRY TRITON
Worldwide, tropical Seas
3 to 4 inches (7.5 to 10 cm)

The periostracum, or outer protein layer of the shell is particularly well developed in this species, as it is in many members of the family Ranellidae.

Plate 76
Cymatium lotorium (Linné, 1758)
[top]
BLACK-SPOTTED TRITON
Tropical Indian and Pacific Oceans
3 to 4 inches (7.5 to 10 cm)

and *Cymatium pyrum* (Linné, 1758)
[bottom]
PEAR TRITON
Tropical Indian and Pacific Oceans
3 inches (7.5 cm)

These predatory animals feed primarily on other gastropods, including venomous cone shells. Snails that are active hunters detect their prey by sense of smell, scanning their siphons from side to side until the direction of the prey is determined. They then follow the scent to their prey.

Plate 77
Cymatium rubeculum (Linné, 1758)
[top]
ROBIN REDBREAST TRITON
Tropical Indian and Pacific Oceans
1.5 inches (4 cm)

and *Cymatium hepaticum* Röding, 1798
[bottom]
BLACK-STRIPED TRITON
Tropical Indian and Pacific Oceans
1.5 inches (4 cm)

Found under coral slabs and rocks along reefs below the tide level, these two species are among the smallest of the Ranellidae.

Plate 78
Biplex perca (Perry, 1811)
MAPLE LEAF TRITON
Western Pacific Ocean
2 inches (5 cm)

Snails that burrow in soft bottoms as well as many snails that live on hard substrates grow shells by the steady addition of small increments of shell to the margin of the aperture, and have a smooth regular form. Snails that live on the surface of sandy or muddy bottoms, especially in the tropics where predators abound, tend to reinforce their shells by periodically thickening or flaring the shell edge to form a varix that may be further fortified with spines. Such shells grow in spurts. The snails add shell rapidly and in fixed increments, usually ranging from 1/6 to nearly a complete volution. Each increment is terminated with a varix. Maple Leaf Tritons grow in increments of 1/2 whorl (180°). The broad varices not only offer increased protection from predators, but stabilize the shell in an aperture down orientation.

Plate 79
Distorsio kurzi Petuch and Harasewych, 1980
[dark]
KURZ'S DISTORSIO
Central Philippines
1.5 inches (4 cm)

and *Distorsio clathrata* (Lamarck, 1816)
[light]
ATLANTIC DISTORSIO
Carolinas to Brazil
2.5 inches (6 cm)

The shells of living distorsios are covered with a dense periostracum consisting of long erect hairs. The animals live on bottoms of sand and rubble, and use their extremely long proboscies to feed on burrowing worms. Growth occurs in increments of 2/3 whorl (240°), with the varix taking the form of a broad platelike extension around the aperture that stabilizes the shell in an aperture down orientation.

Family BURSIDAE

Plate 80
Bursa lamarcki (Deshayes, 1853)
[top]
LAMARCK'S FROG SHELL
Southwestern Pacific Ocean
2 inches (5 cm)

and *Bufonaria nobilis* (Reeve, 1844)
[bottom]
NOBLE FROG SHELL
Southwestern Pacific Ocean
2 inches (5 cm)

Like the remotely related distorsios, frog shells have specialized for feeding on burrowing worms. Equipped with a long narrow proboscis, these animals scour rubble bottoms for prey. They may rely more on sense of "taste" or tactile chemoreception, than on smell to detect their prey in churning shallow waters.

PLATE 56

PLATE 57

PLATE 58

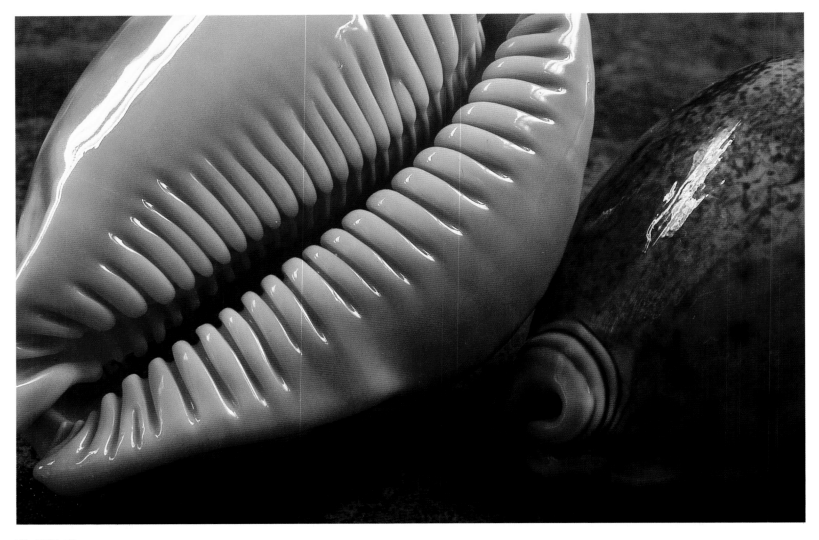

PLATE 59

PLATE 60

PLATE 61

PLATE 62

PLATE 63

PLATE 64

PLATE 65

PLATE 66

PLATE 67

PLATE 68

PLATE 69

PLATE 70

PLATE 71

PLATE 72

PLATE 73

PLATE 74

PLATE 75

PLATE 76

PLATE 77

PLATE 78

PLATE 79

PLATE 80

Family MURICIDAE

Plate 81

Thais planispira (Lamarck, 1822)
EYE-OF-JUDAS ROCK SHELL
Western Mexico to Peru, Galapagos
2 to 3 inches (5 to 7.5 cm)

Muricids are a group of predatory snails characterized by the presence of a specialized organ on the sole of the foot that is capable of dissolving a hole in the calcareous shells of their prey. This adaptation has allowed muricids to feed on animals permanently attached to hard substrates. Such prey, including bivalves and barnacles, is abundant and, by virtue of thick tightly sealed shells, inaccessible to most other predators. Wave-battered rocky shores are rich in prey. Like the limpets and barnacles that inhabit such shores, the Eye-of-Judas Rock Shell has evolved a limpet-like shape.

Plate 82

Drupa rubusidaeus Röding, 1798
STRAWBERRY DRUPE [*large*]
Tropical Indian and Pacific Oceans
1.5 inches (4 cm)

and *Drupa elegans* (Broderip and Sowerby, 1829)
ELEGANT DRUPE [*small*]
Central Polynesia
1 inch (2.5 cm)

Several species of drupes co-occur on tropical coral reefs, but may differ in their location on the reef. The Strawberry Drupe lives on rubble in the breaking surf at the edge of the reef. The Elegant Drupe inhabits calmer midreef areas.

Plate 83

Trophon geversianus (Pallas, 1774)
GEVERS' TROPHON
Southern South America
2 to 4 inches (5 to 10 cm)

This variable species is common on wave-battered, rocky shores where specimens have thick, smooth shells. Thin-shelled, foliated specimens such as the one figured occur in calmer subtidal habitats.

Plate 84

Austrotrophon cerrosensis catalinensis Oldroyd, 1927
CATALINA FORRERIA
Southern California
2 to 3 inches (5 to 7.5 cm)

A rare species, the Catalina Forreria is occasionally collected by divers or dredged in depths of about 150 feet (45 meters) on rocky bottoms.

Plate 85

Poirieria pazi (Crosse, 1869)
[*small*]
PAZ'S MUREX
Tropical western Atlantic Ocean
1.5 inches (4 cm)

and *Poirieria oregonia* Bullis, 1964
[*large*]
R/V OREGON MUREX
Northeast coast of South America
3 inches (7.5 cm)

Except for their larger size, both these species closely resemble 60 million-year-old fossils, and are regarded as among the most primitive members of the family Muricidae. These animals live at 650 feet (200 meters) on sand and fine rubble bottoms. Their spines indicate that they live on the surface of the substrate and do not burrow.

Plate 86

Hexaplex cichoreum (Gmelin, 1791)
ENDIVE MUREX
Southwestern Pacific Ocean
3 to 4 inches (7.5 to 10 cm)

Like many muricids, these animals add shell in increments of 60° and have six varices per volution (hence the genus name *Hexaplex*). Varices are characterized by a general thickening of the shell as well as the presence of a series of recurved spines.

Plate 87

Bolinus brandaris (Linné, 1758)
PURPLE DYE MUREX
Mediterranean Sea
3 to 4 inches (7.5 to 10 cm)

Common throughout the Mediterranean Sea, this species lives in shallow water and feeds on mussels and other bivalves attached to rocks. A gland in the mantle cavity of many muricids produces a secretion that turns dark purple when oxidized. This was one of two common species of muricids gathered since 1,500 B.C. to produce a purple dye used to color the robes of emperors and the aristocracy.

Plate 88

Murex hirasei Hirase, 1915
HIRASE'S MUREX
Japan and Taiwan
2 to 3 inches (5 to 7.5 cm)

These predatory snails live on sandy bottoms at depths of 320 to 650 feet (100 to 200 meters). When not hunting, they are completely buried with only the tip of the siphon protruding above the sand surface like a snorkel. Adaptations for burrowing include a smooth, streamlined shell in which the varices of succeeding whorls are precisely aligned, and a straight, axially oriented siphonal canal.

Plate 89

Murex pecten Lightfoot, 1786
VENUS COMB MUREX
Indian and Pacific Oceans
4 to 6 inches (10 to 15 cm)

The varices and siphonal canal of the Venus Comb Murex are covered with long, thin, closely-spaced, recurved spines that prevent this species from burrowing in the fine sand and mud bottoms on which it lives. The snail extends its tall columnar body, raising the shell until the spines are clear of the bottom, and then crawls forward in search of prey. As the shell grows, the mantle edge dissolves the bases of the spines that obstruct the aperture and siphonal canal.

Plate 90

Chicoreus palmarosae (Lamarck, 1822)
ROSE-BRANCH MUREX
Sri Lanka and southwestern Pacific
3 to 4 inches (7.5 to 10 cm)

This species differs substantially throughout its range. The long spines suffused with pink are characteristic of specimens from Sri Lanka. Philippine specimens have shorter spines and are dark brown in color.

Plate 91

Chicoreus maurus (Broderip, 1833)
MAURUS MUREX
Central Pacific Ocean
3 inches (7.5 cm)

The Maurus Murex, a central Pacific relative of the Rose-Branch Murex, has evolved a stouter, thicker shell with shorter spines and siphonal canal. The animal also produces a hump or node between adjacent varices. These differences are defensive adaptations against predation by crabs and lobsters, which peel back the shell in order to reach the animal.

Plate 92

Pterynotus elongatus (Lightfoot, 1786)
[four specimens]
CLUB MUREX
Tropical Indian and Pacific Oceans
2 to 3 inches (5 to 7.5 cm)

and *Pterynotus pellucidus* (Reeve, 1845)
[lower left, two at 6 & 7 o'clock]
TRANSLUCENT MUREX
Tropical Indian and Pacific Oceans
2 inches (5 cm)

The Club Murex lives on coral rubble along the outer edges of reefs, while the Translucent Murex inhabits sandy patches in deeper waters. Both species are normally white, although occasional specimens of the Club Murex may be suffused with pastel shades of yellow, pink, orange, purple or brown. The infrequent and often irregular coloration may be the result of the snail incorporating unmetabolized pigments from its prey into its own shell.

Plate 93

Pterynotus orchidifloris Shikama, 1973
ORCHID MUREX
Tropical western Pacific Ocean
1 to 1.5 inches (2.5 to 4 cm)

This small shell with broad varices inhabits fine sand and mud bottoms at depths of 160 feet (50 meters) or more. Judging by the relative size of the aperture, the shell is massive compared to the animal. The broad flaring varices may keep the shell above the soft substrate, serving a function similar to that of snowshoes.

Plate 94

Pterynotus bednalli (Brazier, 1878)
BEDNALL'S MUREX
Northern Australia
2 to 3 inches (5 to 7.5 cm)

This is a shallow water species that prefers calm, protected habitats. It lives under large coral slabs and ledges. The broad, flaring varices extend considerably beyond the comparatively small animal, and may function to stabilize the shell relative to the coral slab, providing a protected area in which the animal can feed.

Plate 95

Siratus alabaster (Reeve, 1845)
ALABASTER MUREX
Japan to the Philippines
6 to 8 inches (15 to 20 cm)

The broad webbing of the shell of this species not only stabilizes the orientation of the shell on soft bottoms, but also protects the flanks and rear of the extended foot against attack by predators.

Plate 96

Homalocantha anatomica (Perry, 1811)
ANATOMICAL MUREX
Tropical Indian and Pacific Oceans

Presumably named for its resemblance to a skeleton, the Anatomical Murex, is normally pure white throughout its broad geographic range. Specimens from Hawaii, however, are occasionally brightly colored. The animals live on coral heads at depths of 65 feet (20 meters) and more.

Plate 97

Homalocantha anomliae Kosuge, 1979
ANOMALOUS MUREX
Central Philippines
2 inches (5 cm)

The frail, gossamer nature of this shell indicates that it lives above the substrate in calm waters. It is unlikely that this shell is the animal's only defense against predators.

Plate 98
Murexiella hidalgoi (Crosse, 1869)
[*two specimens on right*]
HIDALGO'S MUREX
Tropical western Atlantic Ocean
1 inch (2.5 cm)

and *Murexiella bojadorensis* Locard, 1897
[*one specimen on left*]
BOJADOR MUREX
Central western Africa
2 inches (5 cm)

These closely related species live at opposite sides of the Atlantic Ocean. Hidalgo's Murex occurs among rubble at depths of 650 feet (200 meters), while the Bojador Murex is taken in shallower water.

Plate 99
Ceratostoma burnetti (Adams and Reeve, 1849)
BURNETT'S MUREX
Korea
3 to 4 inches (7.5 to 10 cm)

Snails of the genus *Ceratostoma* feed on barnacles. The labial tooth, a long spike-like structure emerging from the outer lip, is used to pry open the barnacles. A diet of barnacles and a labial tooth have independently evolved several times among the predatory gastropods.

Plate 100
Ceratostoma foliata (Gmelin, 1791)
FOLIATED THORN PURPURA
Alaska to Southern California

This specimen is indicative of the degree to which many shells are encrusted by other organisms, and illustrates how little of the shell's color or pattern is visible during the animal's lifetime.

Plate 101
Typhinellus occlusus (Garrard, 1963)
BLOCKED TYPHIS
Philippines to eastern Australia
1.5 inches (4 cm)

Typhis shells are characterized by long, tube-like, exhalant as well as inhalant canals. These animals spend considerable time buried, with only the tips of these tubes projecting above the surface of the sand or mud. When a new varix is added, the inner end of the old exhalant tube is sealed off from within the shell. The long, fragile outer tube usually breaks away.

Plate 102
Trubatsa pavlova (Iredale, 1936)
PAVLOVA TYPHIS
Southeastern Australia
1 inch (2.5 cm)

An unusual species that was imaginatively, if anthropomorphically, named to honor a great ballerina.

Family CORALLIOPHILIDAE

Plate 103
Rapa rapa (Linné, 1758)
RAPA SNAIL
Southwestern Pacific Ocean
2 to 3 inches (5 to 7.5 cm)

The family Coraliophillidae is an early offshoot from muricid stock that became specialized for feeding on corals. All have lost their radulae, and feed by sucking the fluids of coral polyps. The Rapa Snail feeds on shallow-water soft corals, and becomes embedded in their bases.

Plate 104
Coralliobia fimbriata (A. Adams, 1854)
FRINGED CORAL SHELL
Tropical Indian and Pacific Oceans
1 inch (2.5 cm)

This species lives and feeds on broad, flat branched coral. It approaches the limpet form by producing a broadly flared lip.

Plate 105
Latiaxis pilsbryi Hirase, 1908
PILSBRY'S LATIAXIS
Japan to South China Sea
1 to 2 inches (2.5 to 5 cm)

This fragile deep water species lives on hard corals at depths of 165 to 650 feet (50 to 200 meters).

Plate 106
Babelomurex spinosus (Hirase, 1908)
SPINY LATIAXIS
Japan to northwestern Australia
1 inch (2.5 cm)

The comparatively large number of species in this genus may be due to a high degree of host specificity. The free-swimming larvae will only metamorphose when in contact with an acceptable host coral.

Plate 107
Babelomurex santacruzensis (Emerson and D'Attilio, 1970)
GALAPAGOS LATIAXIS
Galapagos
1.5 to 2 inches (4 to 5 cm)

Little is known of the biology or habitat of this deep water species. The presence of long spines suggests that it crawls freely on the surface of a hard coral host.

Plate 108
Babelomurex deburghiae (Reeve, 1857)
DEBURGH'S LATIAXIS
Western Pacific Ocean
1.5 inch (4 cm)

The unusual yellow color of this specimen may be indicative of its association with a yellow soft coral.

PLATE 81

PLATE 82

PLATE 83

PLATE 84

PLATE 85

PLATE 86

PLATE 87

PLATE 88

PLATE 89

PLATE 90

PLATE 91

PLATE 92

PLATE 93

PLATE 94

PLATE 95

112

PLATE 96

PLATE 97

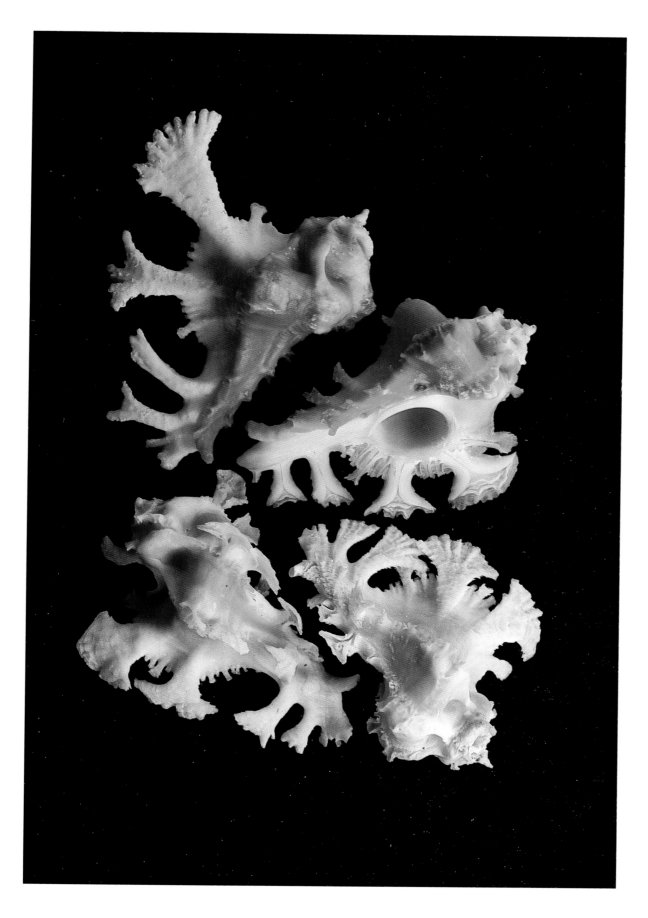

PLATE 98

PLATE 99

PLATE 100

PLATE 101

PLATE 102

PLATE 103

PLATE 104

PLATE 105

PLATE 106

PLATE 107

PLATE 108

Family COLUMBELLIDAE

Plate 109
Columbella haemastoma Sowerby, 1832
BLOOD-STAINED DOVE SHELL
Sea of Cortez to Ecuador and the Galapagos
1 inch (2.5 cm)

Like most members of the genus, this species lives under large rocks and along shallow water rubble bottoms. The long, narrow, thickened aperture is a defense against predation by crabs that feed on the retracted animal after peeling back its shell.

Family BUCCINIDAE

Plate 110
Volutopsius melonis (Dall, 1891)
APPLE BUCCINUM
Bering Sea
4 inches (10 cm)

This species lives at depths of several hundred feet on a bottom of fine mud. Most specimens are white. The purplish coloration of this individual may have been derived from the indigo-colored brittle stars found in the snail's stomach and intestines.

Plate 111
Neptunea polycostata Scarlato, 1952
MANY-RIBBED NEPTUNE
Off northern Japan
5 to 8 inches (12.5 to 20 cm)

Neptunes are large predators that live on hard rubble bottoms, often at considerable depths. The salivary glands of a closely related North Atlantic species have been found to produce a curare-like muscle relaxant, presumably used to anesthetize potential prey. Like most neptunes and whelks, this species also feeds on carrion, and is occasionally taken in baited crab and lobster traps.

Plate 112
Ancistrolepis grammatus (Dall, 1907)
LINED WHELK
Japan
3 inches (7.5 cm)

The thick periostracum and thin, chalky shell are typical features of snails that live in deep water or polar regions, where calcium is in limited supply. The corrugated surface increases the shell's resistance to predators that crush the shell.

Plate 113
Babylonia areolata (Link, 1807)
[top]
AREOLA BABYLON
Taiwan to Sri Lanka
2.5 inches (6 cm)

Babylonia spirata (Linné, 1758)
[left]
SPIRAL BABYLON
Indian Ocean
2.5 inches (6 cm)

Babylonia zeylanica (Brugière, 1789)
[right]
INDIAN BABYLON
East coast of India and Sri Lanka
2 to 3 inches (5 to 7.5 cm)

Like many sand-dwelling buccinids, babylon shells are primarily scavengers, feeding on carrion. Several species are eaten in the Orient, where these snails are trapped in bamboo baskets baited with dead fish.

Plate 114
Volutharpa perryi (Jay, 1855)
PERRY'S VOLUTHARP
Northern Japan to the Bering Sea
1 to 2 inches (2.5 to 5 cm)

Contrary to its name, this species is neither a volute nor a harp, but a buccinid. In polar waters, where calcium availability is limited, the geometry of a shell is greatly influenced by the environment. Similar shell shapes have evolved independently in a number of unrelated snails, making identification even to the family level difficult without dissection.

Plate 115
Godfreyna torri Verco, 1909
TORR'S WHELK
Western Australia
2 inches (5 cm)

The overall shape of this shell bears striking resemblance to that of Cooper's Nutmeg (plate 144), although the coloration differs considerably. While not closely related, both are rapid and efficient burrowers in fine sand bottoms.

Family MELONGENIDAE

Plate 116
Pugilina cochlidium (Linné, 1758)
SPIRAL MELONGENA
Indian Ocean
3 to 4 inches (7.5 to 10 cm)

When inactive, these large common scavengers are at least partially buried in mangroves and sand and mud flats exposed by the tides. Melongenas are active foragers, capable of reaching into deep burrows or other inaccessible areas with their extremely long, slender probosces. Although most apparently prefer to feed on carrion, specimens have been observed to capture and eat other mollusks.

Plate 117
Busycon carica (Gmelin, 1791)
[*left*]
KNOBBED WHELK
Eastern United States
6 to 7 inches (15 to 17.5 cm)

and *Busycon perversum* (Linné, 1758)
[*right*]
PERVERSE WHELK
Yucatan Peninsula
7 to 18 inches (17.5 to 45 cm)

Like the vast majority of snails, the Knobbed Whelk is helically coiled in a right-handed direction, with the aperture to the right of the coiling axis. Although rare, mutations with reversed coiling occur sporadically in a wide variety of snails. Such mutants may survive but normally do not reproduce, since their anatomically asymmetrical bodies are also mirror images of their right-handed counterparts, and therefore incapable of mating with them. The Perverse Whelk is normally left-handed, the species a product of a fortuitous encounter between two mutant left-handed whelks.

Family NASSARIIDAE

Plate 118
Nassarius arcularius (Linné, 1758)
CAKE NASSA
Central and southwestern Pacific Ocean
1 inch (2.5 cm)

Like most nassariids, this species lives in the zone between the tides, where it burrows in sand and mud. Primarily scavengers, the animals emerge from the sand during the change of tides and forage for carrion. The animals have siphons as long as the shell. These are extended and retracted through a notch in the rounded anterior of the shell, rather than enclosed in a permanent siphonal canal.

Family FASCIOLARIIDAE

Plate 119
Colubraria tortuosa (Reeve, 1844)
TWISTED DWARF TRITON
Indian and western Pacific Oceans
1.5 inches (4 cm)

The Twisted Dwarf Triton adds shell in increments of just under a complete volution. The tangential alignment of the varices accounts for the spirally distorted apex of the shell.

Family OLIVIDAE

Plate 120
Oliva incrassata Lightfoot, 1786
ANGLED OLIVE
Gulf of California to Peru
2.5 inches (6 cm)

Oliva irisans Lamarck, 1811
IRIS OLIVE
Ryukyu Islands to northern Australia
2 inches (5 cm)

Oliva vidua (Röding, 1798)
BLACK OLIVE
Tropical Indian and Pacific Oceans
2 inches (5 cm)

Oliva circinata tostesi Petuch, 1987
TOSTES' OLIVE
Brazil
2 inches (5 cm)

Oliva bulbosa Röding, 1798
INFLATED OLIVE
Tropical Indian Ocean
2 inches (5 cm)

Oliva rubrolabiata Fischer, 1902
RED-LIPPED OLIVE
New Hebrides, New Caledonia and Solomon Islands
2 inches (5 cm)

Oliva peruviana Lamarck, 1811
PERUVIAN OLIVE
Peru and Chile
2 inches (5 cm)

Oliva miniacea (Röding, 1798)
RED-MOUTHED OLIVE
Tropical Indian and Pacific Oceans
2.5 inches (6 cm)

Oliva tremulina flammeacolor Petuch and Sargent, 1986
FLAME-COLORED OLIVE
Southern India
2 inches (5 cm)

Oliva caerulea ponderi Petuch and Sargent, 1986
PONDER'S OLIVE
Western Australia
2 inches (5 cm)

The elongate, streamlined shape of olive shells readily identifies them as rapid burrowers in sandy and muddy bottoms. Like many groups that have adapted to this habitat, they no longer have an operculum. The forward portion of their long broad foot is expanded to form a plow-like baffle that further improves the efficiency of burrowing. Many species live in large colonies, with thousands of specimens occurring on a single tidal sand bar. Although willing to feed on carrion, olives hunt other mollusks, especially smaller snails and bivalves.

Plate 120
1. *Oliva incrassata*
2. *Oliva irisans*
3. *Oliva vidua*
4. *Oliva circinata tostesi*
5. *Oliva bulbosa*
6. *Oliva rubrolabiata*
7. *Oliva peruviana*
8. *Oliva mineacea*
9. *Oliva tremulina flammeacolor*
10. *Oliva caerulea ponderi*

Plate 121
Oliva porphyria (Linné, 1758)
TENT OLIVE
Sea of Cortez to Panama
2 to 5 inches

The tent-like markings on this, the largest of the living olives, are but one form of the extremely variable chevron patterns that occur in a wide-ranging variety of shallow water snails (plates 156, 157) and bivalves (plate 200).

Plate 122
Ancilla lienardi Bernardi, 1821
LIENARD'S ANCILLA
Brazil
1 to 2 inches

Closely related to the olives, the ancillas are also specialized for a burrowing habitat. The animal completely envelops the shell with lateral extensions of its mantle.

Family MITRIDAE

Plate 123
Mitra mitra (Linné, 1758)
EPISCOPAL MITER
Tropical Indian and Pacific Oceans
4 inches (10 cm)

Mitra papalis Linné, 1758)
PAPAL MITER
Tropical Indian and Pacific Oceans
2 inches (5 cm)

and *Mitra stictica* (Link, 1807)
PONTIFICAL MITER
Tropical Indian and Pacific Oceans
2.5 inches (6 cm)

Like the olives, miters are well adapted for burrowing in soft bottoms. Many species live in clean coralline sand at the bases of reefs. Animals tend to be nocturnal and feed on sipunculids, known commonly as peanutworms.

Plate 124
Vexillum regina filiaregina J. Cate, 1961
[*orange*]
COLORFUL QUEEN VEXILLUM
Philippines
2.5 inches (6 cm)

and *Vexillum taeniatum* (Lamarck, 1811)
[*yellow*]
RIBBONED VEXILLUM
Tropical Indian and Pacific Oceans
2 inches (5 cm)

Although related to the miters, the vexillums differ considerably in shell structure as well as anatomical organization. Also sand dwellers, several vexillums have been reported to feed on small crustaceans.

Family TURBINELLIDAE

Plate 125
Vasum cassiforme (Kiener, 1841)
HELMET VASE
Northeastern Brazil
2 to 4 inches (5 to 10 cm)

All members of the family Turbinellidae have become highly adapted for feeding on burrowing worms. Vase shells live among coral rubble, and have an extremely long, extendable proboscis with which they reach deep into crevices and burrows to capture polychaete worms. Their shells are extremely thick and heavy, although several species such as the Helmet Vase, which live in calmer, deeper waters, have spiny shells.

Plate 126
Tudivasum armigera (A. Adams, 1855)
ARMORED VASE
Western Australia
2 to 4 inches (5 to 10 cm)

Like the Helmet Vase, the Armored Vase lives in deeper (65 to 165 feet/20 to 50 meters), offshore waters. The long spines increase the effective volume of the shell, and may serve as a defense against predators such as fish, which swallow their prey.

Plate 127
Columbarium harrisae Harasewych, 1980
HARRIS' PAGODA SHELL
Eastern Australia
4 to 5 inches (10 to 12.5 cm)

Like all living members of this group, Harris' Pagoda Shell is restricted to the deeper waters along the continental slope. This species most closely resembles a 40 million-year-old fossil form that lived in the shallow coastal waters of the southeastern United States.

Plate 128
Coluzea juliae Harasewych, 1989
JULIA'S PAGODA SHELL
Southeastern Africa
3 to 4 inches (7.5 to 10 cm)

Pagoda shells live on sand and rubble bottoms, feeding on tube-dwelling polychaete worms by extending their extremely long and slender prosces down into the worm's tube. Most do not burrow to any appreciable degree.

Plate 129
Coluzea aapta Harasewych, 1986
UNAPPROACHABLE PAGODA SHELL
Western Australia
2 inches (5 cm)

Shells of living animals of this species are often covered by as many as seven or eight anemones, making it unapproachable indeed.

PLATE 109

PLATE 110

PLATE 111

PLATE 112

PLATE 113

PLATE 114

PLATE 115

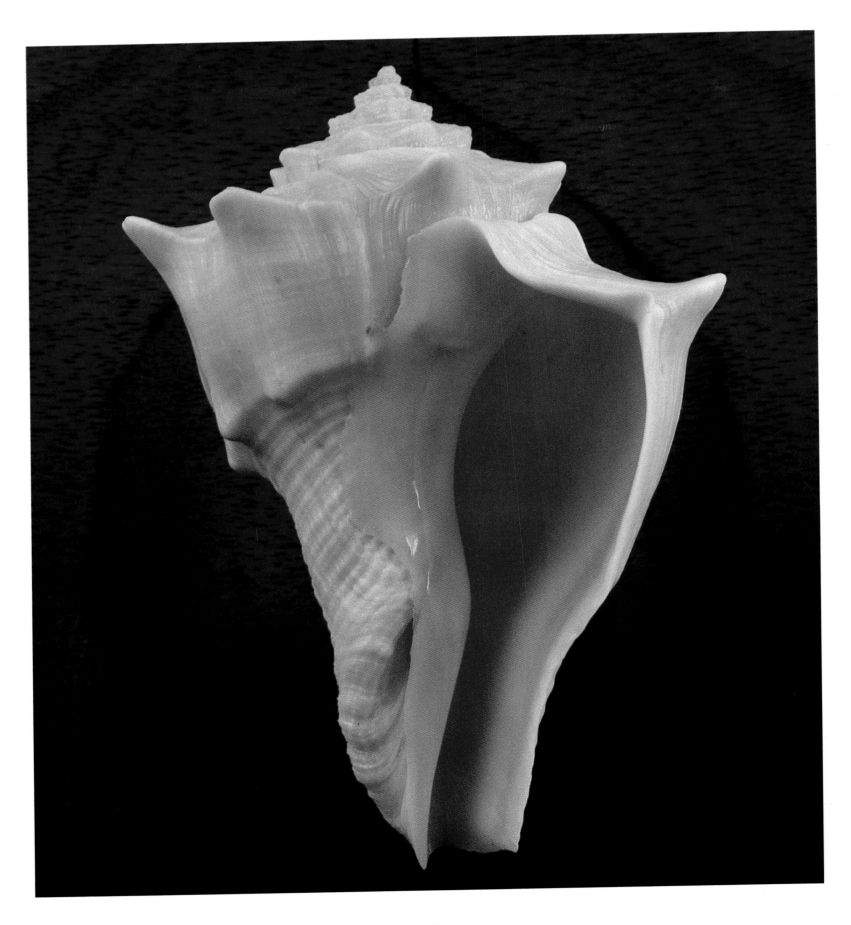

PLATE 116

PLATE 117

PLATE 118

PLATE 119

PLATE 120

PLATE 121

PLATE 122

PLATE 123

PLATE 124

PLATE 125

PLATE 126

PLATE 127

PLATE 128   PLATE 129

Family HARPIDAE

Plate 130
Harpa costata (Linné, 1758)
[*two large*]
IMPERIAL HARP SHELL
Mauritius
3 inches (7.5 cm)

and *Harpa doris* Röding, 1798
[*two small*]
DORIS HARP
Western Africa and Cape Verde Islands
2.5 inches (6 cm)

These large, shallow-water predators feed on small crabs and shrimp, which they envelop and smother with their broad foot. Although the shell has a large aperture, the animals lack an operculum, as do many other sand-dwelling snails.

Plate 131
Harpa ventricosa Lamarck, 1816
VENTRAL HARP
Western Indian Ocean and Red Sea
4 inches (10 cm)

Harp snails are able to shed or self-amputate the rear portion of their foot. Like the ability of some lizards to shed their tails, this presumably functions as a distraction to potential predators while the animal escapes.

Plate 132
Morum lindae Petuch, 1987
LINDA'S MORUM
Caribbean Coast off Colombia
1 inch (2.5 cm)

Based on shell architecture, morums were, until recently, considered to be closely related to the bonnet shells (plate 70). Anatomical studies have revealed that their true affinities lie with the harp shells.

Family VOLUTIDAE

Plate 133
Cymbium glans (Gmelin, 1791)
ELEPHANT'S SNOUT
Central Western Africa
10 to 12 inches (25 to 30 cm)

Among the most ancient of predatory snails, the volutes are confined to sand and mud bottoms from the tropics to the poles. These large and aggressive hunters feed mainly on other snails, which they envelop with their foot. Although they hunt on the surface, volutes will often burrow to consume their prey beneath the sand.

Plate 134
Cymbiola aulica (Sowerby, 1825)
PRINCELY VOLUTE
Southern Philippines
4 to 6 inches (10 to 15 cm)

This species is among the most variable of volutes. The large larval shells are indicative of young that undergo metamorphosis within the egg capsule and emerge as crawling miniatures of the adults. There is little interbreeding between populations, allowing distinctive characters to accumulate rapidly in small local populations.

Plate 135
Cymbiola deshayesi (Reeve, 1855)
DESHAYES' VOLUTE
New Caledonia
3 inches (7.5 cm)

This species, closely related to the Princely Volute, occurs only along the northern coast of New Caledonia. Its limited range may account for the small degree of variation in its shell.

Plates 136/137
Paramoria guntheri (E.A. Smith, 1886)
GUNTHER'S VOLUTE
Southern Australia
2 inches (5 cm)

Unlike the shell, the animal is brightly colored with orange reticulations over its white foot. Gunther's Volute is a denizen of deep water (130 to 260 feet/40 to 80 meters) sand and rubble bottoms.

Plate 138
[*Left to right*]
Scaphella dubia kieneri (Clench, 1946)
KIENER'S VOLUTE
Northern Gulf of Mexico
6 to 8 inches (15 to 20 cm)

Scaphella dubia (Broderip, 1827)
DUBIOUS VOLUTE
Southeastern United States
3 to 4 inches (7.5 to 10 cm)

Scaphella junonia (Lamarck, 1804)
[*two specimens*]
JUNONIA
Southeastern United States
4 to 5 inches (10 to 12.5 cm)

Once worldwide in distribution, this genus of volutes is today restricted to the Tropical western Atlantic, Gulf of Mexico and Caribbean Sea. Some species, such as the Junonia, can be found at depths of 65 feet (20 meters). Others, such as the Dubious Volute, occur at substantially greater depths.

Plate 139
Ampulla priamus (Gmelin, 1791)
SPOTTED FLASK VOLUTE
Portugal to northwestern Africa
2 to 3 inches (5 to 7.5 cm)

Although the shell is thinner and more inflated, this genus, which contains but a single species, is closely related to *Scaphella*. The characteristic color pattern was no doubt inherited from their ancient common ancestor.

Plate 140
Volutoconus bednalli (Brazier, 1878)
BEDNALL'S VOLUTE
Northern Australia
4 to 5 inches (10 to 12.5 cm)

The pattern and coloration of this volute are striking and distinctive when viewed out of the water, but provide camouflage in the sandy sea grass beds on which this species lives.

Plate 141
Zidona palliata Kaiser, 1976
MANTLED VOLUTE
Southern Brazil
4 inches (10 cm)

Unlike most volutes, the animal of this species is capable of completely enveloping the shell in its mantle, producing a glossy overglaze.

Family MARGINELLIDAE

Plate 142
Glabella pseudofaba (Sowerby, 1846)
QUEEN MARGINELLA
Western Africa
1.5 inch (4 cm)

Like the olives and cowries, the marginellas are capable of extending their mantles to completely cover their shells. Little is known of the biology of these tropical, sand-dwelling animals.

Plate 143
Marginella desjardini Marche-Marchad, 1957
DESJARDIN'S MARGINELLA
Western Africa
2 inches (5 cm)

Although several species of marginellas are often encountered feeding on carrion, many have a complex crop and poison gland. Some, including the two species illustrated in plates 142 and 143, lack a radula, suggesting that their prey is swallowed whole.

Family CANCELLARIIDAE

Plate 144
Progabbia cooperi (Gabb, 1865)
COOPER'S NUTMEG SNAIL
Central California south along the outer coast of the Baja Peninsula
2 to 3 inches (5 to 7.5 cm)

These "vampire snails" are normally buried in the sand until a torpedo ray or angel shark settles on the bottom nearby. Then these snails emerge from the sand and converge on the sleeping prey. Extending their long prosboces, they pierce the softer tissues, usually around the gills and mouth, and feed on the blood of the sleeping shark.

Plate 145
Scalptia mercadoi Old, 1968
MERCADO'S NUTMEG
Philippines
1.5 inch (4 cm)

Like many sand-burrowing groups, the nutmeg shells have lost the operculum during their evolution. Unlike most members of the family, the shell of Mercado's Nutmeg has frequent pronounced varices, which impede burrowing but provide increased resistance to predation.

Plate 146
Trigonostoma milleri Burch, 1949
MILLER'S NUTMEG
Costa Rica and Galapagos
1 inch (2.5 cm)

The shell of this nutmeg is always uncoiled, and therefore structurally weak. Although little is known of the biology of this rare species, it may be surmised that it lives in association with another animal that confers additional protection from predators.

Plate 147
Sveltia gladiator (Petit, 1976)
GLADIATOR NUTMEG
Galapagos
2 inches (5 cm)

Although little is known about the food of most nutmeg snails, all members of the family studied thus far have specialized adaptations of the mouth and esophagus that suggest these animals are suctorial predators, consuming body fluids of their prey. The spines of the Gladiator Nutmeg indicate that this species finds its preferred prey on hard substrates rather than on a sandy bottom.

Family TURRIDAE

Plate 148
Turris babylonia (Linné, 1758)
BABYLON TURRID
Tropical Pacific Ocean
3 inches (7.5 cm)

The families Turridae, Conidae and Terebridae are collectively termed Toxoglossa [poison tooth], based on their unusual mode of feeding. All are predators, and many have tubular, harpoonlike teeth with which they impale their prey. A paralytic poison is then injected through the hollow portion of the tooth.

Plate 149/150
Thatcheria mirabilis Angas, 1877
JAPANESE WONDER SHELL
Western Pacific Ocean
3 to 4 inches (7.5 to 10 cm)

The distinctive form of this shell is reputed to have inspired the architecture of the Guggenheim Museum. Once a great rarity, this species is known to occur in abundance on muddy bottoms at depths ranging from 200 to 1,300 feet (60 to 400 meters). The deep sinus at the apical end of the aperture allows a nearly linear flow of water through the mantle cavity.

Family CONIDAE

Plate 151
Conus marmoreus Linné, 1758
MARBLE CONE
Tropical Indian and Pacific Oceans
3 to 4 inches (7.5 to 10 cm)

Although all cones have specialized, harpoon-like radular teeth and well-developed poison glands, they can be divided into three major groups based on diet. The largest and most diverse group feed on polychaete worms. Many of the cones in this category have adapted to feeding on a particular species of worm. Other cones have a diet consisting of other snails. The third, smallest, and presumably most recently evolved group feed on bottom-dwelling fish. "Stings" by some of the larger, fish-eating species have been known to cause human fatalities.

Plate 152
Conus ammiralis Linné, 1758
ADMIRAL CONE
Tropical Indian and western Pacific Oceans
2 inches (5 cm)

Shells with long, narrow apertures and tent-like color patterns are indicative of cones that eat other mollusks. Both the Admiral Cone and the Marble Cone (plate 151) are known to feed on snails. The Thailand Cone (plate 154), Illustrious and Glory-of-India Cones (plate 156) as well as the Glory-of-the-Seas Cone (plate 157) are all inferred to have a similar diet.

Plate 153
Conus thomae Gmelin, 1791
ST. THOMAS CONE
Indonesia, Philippines
3 inches (7.5 cm)

Although several specimens were present in collections made during the 18th century, the habitat of this formerly rare species was rediscovered during the past two decades. Taken at depths of about 330 feet (100 meters), this species is presumed to feed on worms living on sand and rubble bottoms.

Plate 154
Conus colubrinus thailandis da Motta, 1978
THAILAND CONE
Andaman Sea
3 inches (7.5 cm)

This large, heavy cone lives at depths of 30 to 100 feet (10 to 30 meters). Most cones reabsorb the calcium from the inner whorls of the shell until only paper-thin, transparent partitions remain. This both reduces the weight and increases the volume available for internal tissues, without diminishing the protective function of the shell.

Plate 155
Conus stupella (Kuroda, 1956)
STUPELLA CONE
Southern Japan, Taiwan
3 inches (7.5 cm)

Most cones are restricted to tropical waters. A few species occur in Japan, marking the northernmost extent of the range of the family. This rare, deep-water species is presumed to feed on worms.

Plate 156
Conus excelsus Sowerby, 1908
[left]
ILLUSTRIOUS CONE
Western Pacific
3.5 inches (8.5 cm)

and *Conus milneedwardsi* Jousseaume, 1894
[right]
GLORY-OF-INDIA CONE
Indian Ocean
5 inches (12.5 cm)

These two closely related species are descended from a more widely distributed common ancestor. Isolation of the two offshoot populations has resulted in the accumulation of the observed differences in their respective gene pools.

Plate 157
Conus gloriamaris Chemnitz, 1777
GLORY-OF-THE-SEAS CONE
Western Pacific
4 to 6 inches (10 to 15 cm)

Another fabled rarity, this species is now found in considerable numbers throughout the Philippines. Although specimens have been collected intertidally, most live on fine sand bottoms at depths ranging from 65 to 260 feet (20 to 80 meters).

Plate 158
Conus cedonulli Linné, 1758
MATCHLESS CONE
Lesser Antilles
1.5 to 2 inches (4 to 5 cm)

The Matchless Cone, whose Latin name *cedonulli* translates to "I yield to none," was one of the great rarities of the 18th century. Today it is found in moderate numbers throughout the southeastern Caribbean.

Family TEREBRIDAE

Plate 159
[top to bottom]
Terebra strigata Sowerby, 1825
ZEBRA AUGER
Gulf of California to Peru, Galpagos
4 to 5 inches (10 to 12.5 cm)

Terebra areolata (Link, 1807)
FLY-SPOTTED AUGER
Tropical Indian and Pacific Oceans
4 to 5 inches (10 to 12.5 cm)

Duplicaria duplicata (Linné, 1758)
DUPLICATE AUGER
Tropical Indian and western Pacific
Oceans
2 to 3 inches (5 to 7.5 cm)

Terebra maculata (Linné, 1758)
MARLINSPIKE
Tropical Indian and Pacific Oceans
6 to 10 inches (15 to 25 cm)

Terebra felina (Dillwyn, 1817)
TIGER AUGER
Tropical Indian and Pacific Oceans
2 to 3 inches (5 to 7.5 cm)

Terebra dimidiata (Linné, 1758)
DIMIDIATE AUGER
Tropical Indian and Pacific Oceans
4 to 6 inches (10 to 15 cm)

Auger shells are identified as burrowers in sand and mud bottoms by their characteristic shape. Most remain buried during the day and feed at night or during the changing tide. Some species, among them the Fly-Spotted Auger and the Marlinspike, lack a radula. They capture hemicordate worms and swallow them whole. Other species have harpoon-like radular teeth and poison glands, and feed on tube-dwelling polychaete worms.

Plate 160
Terebra triseriata Gray, 1834
TRISERIATE AUGER
Southwestern Pacific Ocean
3 to 4 inches (7.5 to 10 cm)

The most elongate and slender of snails, this species burrows in muddy bottoms. The ratio of shell mass to foot size, the latter estimated from the cross-sectional area of the aperture, may represent a functional limit to mobility.

Family HYDATINIDAE

Plate 161
Hydatina physis Linné, 1758
[three narrow striped]
GREEN-LINED PAPER BUBBLE
Tropical Indian and Pacific Oceans
1 to 1.5 inches (2.5 to 4 cm)

and *Hydatina zonata* (Lightfoot, 1786)
[two broad striped]
ZONE PAPER BUBBLE
Tropical Indian and Pacific Oceans
1 to 1.5 inches (2.5 to 4 cm)

Resembling quail eggs in size and delicacy, these fragile shells offer little protection against predators. The animals are considerably larger, and often more colorful than the shells, which they nearly envelop when crawling. Bubble shells congregate for spawning, and can occasionally be found in large numbers on shallow, calm mud flats.

Family UMBRACULIDAE

Plate 162
Umbraculum umbraculum (Lightfoot, 1786)
[white]
UMBRELLA SHELL
Tropical Indian and Pacific Oceans, Caribbean Sea

and *Umbraculum pictum* A. Adams, 1854
[yellow]
YELLOW UMBRELLA SHELL
Shells to 2 inches (5 cm), animals to 6 inches (15 cm)

These thin shells cover but a small portion of the animal's upper surface, and are usually covered with algae or other encrusting organisms. Animals live in tide pools as well as deeper waters along coral reefs.

Family CAVOLINIDAE

Plate 163
Cuvierina columnella (Rang, 1827)
CIGAR PTEROPOD
[tubular]

Cavolinia uncinata (Rang, 1829)
UNCINATE CAVOLINE
[larger round]

Diacria trispinosa (Blainville, 1821)
THREE-SPINED CAVOLINE
[spiked]

All approximately 0.3 inch (1 cm)
Worldwide, equatorial seas

These small gastropods, commonly called sea butterflies, spend their lives in the plankton, swimming by flapping wing-like projections of the foot. Their shells are greatly reduced in size and weight and, like boat hulls, are bilaterally symmetrical due to hydrodynamic constraints.

PLATE 130

PLATE 131

PLATE 132

PLATE 133

PLATE 134

PLATE 135

PLATE 136

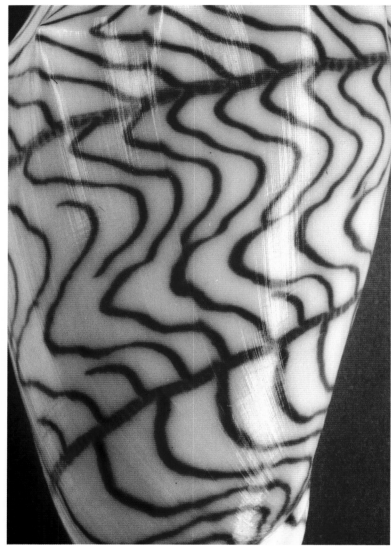

PLATE 137

PLATE 138

PLATE 139

PLATE 140

PLATE 141

PLATE 142

PLATE 143

PLATE 144

PLATE 145

PLATE 146

PLATE 147

PLATE 148

PLATE 150

PLATE 149

PLATE 151

PLATE 152

PLATE 153

PLATE 154

PLATE 155

PLATE 156

PLATE 157

PLATE 158

PLATE 159

PLATE 160

PLATE 161

PLATE 162

PLATE 163

CLASS

CEPHALOPODA

Family NAUTILIDAE

Plate 164
Nautilus macromphalus Sowerby, 1849
[*left*]
NEW CALEDONIA NAUTILUS
New Caledonia
6 to 7 inches (15 to 17.5 cm)

Nautilus pompilius Linné, 1758
[*two middle*]
CHAMBERED NAUTILUS
Southwestern Pacific Ocean
6 to 8 inches (15 to 20 cm)

Nautilus scrobiculatus Lightfoot, 1786
[*right*]
UMBILICATE NAUTILUS
New Guinea and Solomon Islands
6 to 7 inches (15 to 17.5 cm)

There are but a few living species of this ancient and once diverse group of cephalopods. The nautiluses occur primarily in deep water (650 to 1,300 feet/200 to 400 meters) along the outer edges of coral reefs. These free swimming animals feed on fish and shrimp, which they capture with their tentacles.

Plate 165
Nautilus pompilius Linné, 1758
CHAMBERED NAUTILUS
Southwestern Pacific Ocean
6 to 8 inches (15 to 20 cm)

These sections, cut parallel to the plane of symmetry, reveal the internal structure of the nautilus shell. The section in the center of the plate shows the position of the siphuncle tube on the simply curved septa. Only the calcified portions of the siphuncle are visible in this photograph. In the living animal, these are connected by a membranous tube.

Family AMALTHEIDAE

Plate 166
Amaltheus margaritatus de Montfort, 1808
PEARLY AMMONITE
Germany, Lower Jurassic
1.5 inches (4 cm)

The calcified shell of this fossil ammonite has gradually been replaced by pyrite or fool's gold. This sectioned specimen reveals the septa and portions of the siphuncle, which was situated along the outer rim of the chambers.

Family PLACENTICERATIDAE

Plate 167/168
Placenticeras meeki Boehm, 1898
MEEK'S AMMONITE
South Dakota, 65–100 million years old
10 inches (25 cm)

Unlike nautiloids, which had fairly simple septa or partitions between adjacent chambers, the septa of ammonites became increasingly complex. The closeup of Meek's Ammonite (plate 168) shows portions of several adjacent septa.

Family SPIRULIDAE

Plate 169
Spirula spirula (Linné, 1758)
COMMON SPIRULA
Worldwide, warm seas
1 inch (2.5 cm)

Like the nautilus and the ammonites, this small shell contains gas-filled chambers joined by a siphuncle. However, the shell of the Common Spirula, a small deep-sea squid, is completely internal. These animals float with shell uppermost and tentacles downward at depths in excess of 3,300 feet (1,000 meters).

Family OMMASTREPHIDAE

Plate 170
Illex illecebrosus (Lesueur, 1821)
COMMON SHORT-FINNED SQUID
Northwestern Atlantic, Newfoundland to Florida
12 to 18 inches for the entire animal, 6 to 10 inches for the pen or gladius

Flexible and transparent, these feather-like pens or gladii are all that remain of the shell in free-swimming squid. Completely internal, the gladius contributes rigidity to the elongate tubular body.

Family ARGONAUTIDAE

Plate 171
Argonauta argo (Linné, 1758)
[*larger white specimens*]
COMMON PAPER NAUTILUS
Worldwide, warm seas
6 to 8 inches (15 to 20 cm)

and *Argonauta hians* Lightfoot, 1786
[*smaller brown specimens*]
BROWN PAPER NAUTILUS
Warmer regions of the Atlantic and Pacific Oceans
1.5 to 2.5 inches (4 to 6 cm)

These elaborate egg cases are secreted by specialized tentacles of female octopods belonging to the genus *Argonauta*. They cannot be considered true shells, since they are not produced by the mantle. The female carries the egg case, much as the Chambered Nautilus carries its shell, until the eggs hatch. Similar hydrodynamic constraints rather than common descent are responsible for the convergence in form.

PLATE 164

PLATE 165

PLATE 166

PLATE 167

PLATE 168

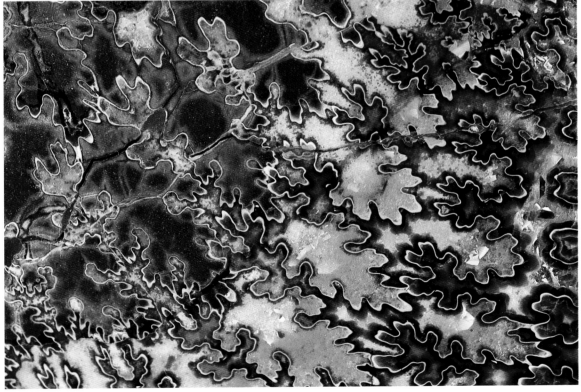

PLATE 169

PLATE 170

PLATE 171

CLASS
BIVALVIA

Family NUCULANIDAE

Plate 172
Nuculana fastigata Keen, 1958
EXALTED NUT CLAM
Gulf of California to Peru
0.5 to 1 inch (1 to 2.5 cm)

Among the most primitive of bivalves, these animals live in soft muddy bottoms and feed by ingesting sediment rather than on material filtered from the seawater by their gills. The broad, deeply corrugated hinge area assures stable alignment of the two valves of the shell.

Family CUCULAEIDAE

Plate 173
Cucullaea labiata (Lightfoot, 1786)
HOODED ARK
Southwestern Pacific Ocean
2 to 3 inches (5 to 7.5 cm)

A small brittle star (ophiuroid) must have found its way beneath the mantle edge of this Hooded Ark, and was covered with shell material. The outline of this brittle star is still visible in the blister pearl on the left valve (lower left). Only pearls formed by mollusks that produce nacre, a particular crystalline form of calcium carbonate, are lustrous.

Family LIMOPSIDAE

Plate 174
Limopsis marionensis E. A. Smith, 1885
MARION LIMOPSIS
Antarctica
1 to 1.5 inches (2.5 to 4 cm)

Limopsis occur primarily in cold water, either in polar regions or at considerable depths. These bivalves have a thick, velvety periostracum made of protein that protects the shell from abrasion and/or dissolution. The frilly edge overhangs the shell gape and keeps sand and gravel from entering the mantle cavity.

Family ARCIDAE

Plate 175
Trisodis yongei
YONGE'S TWISTED ARK
Southwestern Pacific Ocean
2 to 3 inches (5 to 7.5 cm)

These bivalves live partially buried in the sand, and are attached to buried rocks or rubble by means of numerous hair-like strands, collectively termed a byssus. Due to the twisted form, the portion of the shell that is above the sand surface lies in the plane of the surface. This allows the shell to expand, producing a greater separation of inhalant and exhalant openings to the mantle cavity, while maintaining a low profile that offers little resistance to currents.

Family MYTILIDAE

Plate 176
Perna viridis (Linné, 1758)
GREEN MUSSEL
Southwestern Pacific and Indian Oceans
2 inches (5 cm)

Like the ark shells, mussels are attached to hard substrates such as rocks or pilings by byssal threads. The byssus is attached at the anterior end of the shell, which is much reduced in size. The posterior end, containing the gills, is greatly enlarged. Shells tend to be triangular in cross-section, with the flat base adjacent to the substrate in order to stabilize the shell.

Family PINNIDAE

Plate 177
Atrina rigida (Lightfoot, 1786)
STIFF PEN SHELL
Tropical western Atlantic and Caribbean
6 to 10 inches (15 to 25 cm)

The triangular shell is buried, apex down, with the base just extending above the surface of sandy bottoms. Major organs are small and situated in the lowermost portions of the shell, beyond the reach of many predators. The exposed portions of the shell are frequently damaged and rapidly repaired. Byssal threads are long and silky, and have been woven into fabric by Mediterranean cultures for millennia. The "Golden Fleece" of Greek mythology may have been made of spun pen shell byssus.

Family PTERIIDAE

Plate 178
Electroma zebra (Reeve, 1859)
ZEBRA-STRIPED WING OYSTER
Southwestern Pacific Ocean
0.6 inch (1.5 cm)

The dark brown bands on this small wing oyster match in thickness, orientation and color the branches of the soft coral on which it lives. Protective coloration is a defense, primarily against vertebrate predators, as most invertebrates hunt by smell rather than sight.

Family MALLEIDAE

Plate 179
Malleus malleus (Linné, 1758)
COMMON HAMMER OYSTER
Tropical Indian and Pacific Oceans
8 inches (20 cm)

Unlike true oysters, these bivalves live on sandy bottoms. The hammer-like expansions of the hinge serve to stabilize the shell and prevent it from being turned over.

Family LIMIDAE

Plate 180
Acesta rathbuni (Bartsch, 1913)
RATHBUN'S GIANT LIMA
Philippines
4 to 6 inches (10 to 15 cm)

Members of the family Limidae are capable of swimming, and trail long sensory tentacles from the mantle margin. Limas commonly build cocoon-like nests in rocky rubble, connecting adjacent pieces with byssal threads.

Family OSTREIDAE

Plate 181
Lopha cristagalli (Linné, 1758)
COCK'S-COMB OYSTER
Tropical Indian and Pacific Oceans
3 to 4 inches (7.5 to 10 cm)

The zig-zag margin of these attached bivalves insures proper alignment of the valves and limits prying and crushing predation.

Plate 182
Crassostrea gigas (Thunberg, 1793)
GIANT PACIFIC OYSTER
Northern Pacific Ocean
3 to 10 inches (7.5 to 25 cm)

Free-swimming oyster larvae settle on a suitable hard bottom, and cement their left valve to the substrate. The lower valve becomes deeper, the upper valve flatter. As in gastropods that permanently cement their shells to substrate (plate 33), the shape of the shell is governed more by the substrate, including such factors as adjacent organisms and current than by considerations of strict symmetry. The figured specimens were grown on an "oyster farm," suspended in calm, nutrient-rich water, and are more symmetrical than oysters that grow in the wild.

Family PECTINIDAE

Plate 183
Cryptopecten pallium (Linné, 1758)
ROYAL CLOAK SCALLOP
Indian and Pacific Oceans
2 inches (5 cm)

Chlamys senatoria nobilis (Reeve, 1852)
NOBLE SCALLOP
Japan
3 inches (7.5 cm)

Lyropecten subnodosus (Sowerby, 1825)
PACIFIC LION'S PAW
Gulf of California to Peru
5 inches (12.5 cm)

Scallops are among the few bivalves that are capable of swimming. By rapidly closing their shells, they produce a jet of water that propels them off the bottom. Species that lie freely on sand or rubble bottoms swim frequently. Others are normally attached to rocks by a byssus and swim only rarely. As juveniles, all scallops are byssally attached.

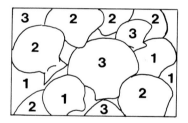

Plate 183
1. *Cryptopecten pallium*
2. *Chlamys senatoria nobilis*
3. *Lyropecten subnodosus*

Plate 184

Somalipecten cranmerorum Waller, 1986
CRANMER'S SCALLOP
Somalia
2 to 3 inches (5 to 7.5 cm)

This recently discovered species lives in 490 to 980 feet (150 to 300 meters) of water. The uniform distribution of encrusting organisms over the outer surfaces of the shell indicates that this species is attached by a byssus to rocks and rubble, and does not lie on soft bottoms.

Plate 185

Lyropecten nodosus (Linné, 1758)
LION'S PAW
Carolinas to Brazil
3 to 6 inches (7.5 to 15 cm)

The corrugated shell surface of many scallops serves to increase the strength of the shell without increasing its weight. This is an important consideration for swimming species.

Family PROPEAMUSSIIDAE

Plate 186

Propeamussium dalli (E. A. Smith, 1886)
DALL'S GLASS SCALLOP
Gulf of Mexico and Caribbean
1 to 2 inches (2.5 to 5 cm)

These deep water scallops are extremely thin and delicate. Although their exterior surfaces are smooth, they have internal ribs, visible through the transparent shell, that provide structural support.

Family SPONDYLIDAE

Plate 187

Spondylus sinensis Schreibers, 1793
CHINESE THORNY OYSTER
Tropical western Pacific Ocean
2 to 3 inches (5 to 7.5 cm) excluding spines

Although commonly categorized as thorny oysters, these bivalves are closely related to scallops. Juveniles look like tiny scallops, and attach to hard substrate by a byssus. As they grow, the animals cement their right valve to the substrate, and produce thick, spiny shells.

Plate 188

Spondylus americanus Hermann, 1781
AMERICAN THORNY OYSTER
Carolinas to Brazil
3 to 4 inches (7.5 to 10 cm) excluding spines

This species is most often collected from wrecks at depths ranging from 80 to 165 feet (25 to 50 meters). In their native habitat, the shells are so overgrown with algae and encrusting organisms as to hardly be recognizable. Specimens with long spines occur in calm, protected waters.

PLATE 172

PLATE 173

PLATE 174

PLATE 175

PLATE 176

PLATE 177

PLATE 178

186

PLATE 179

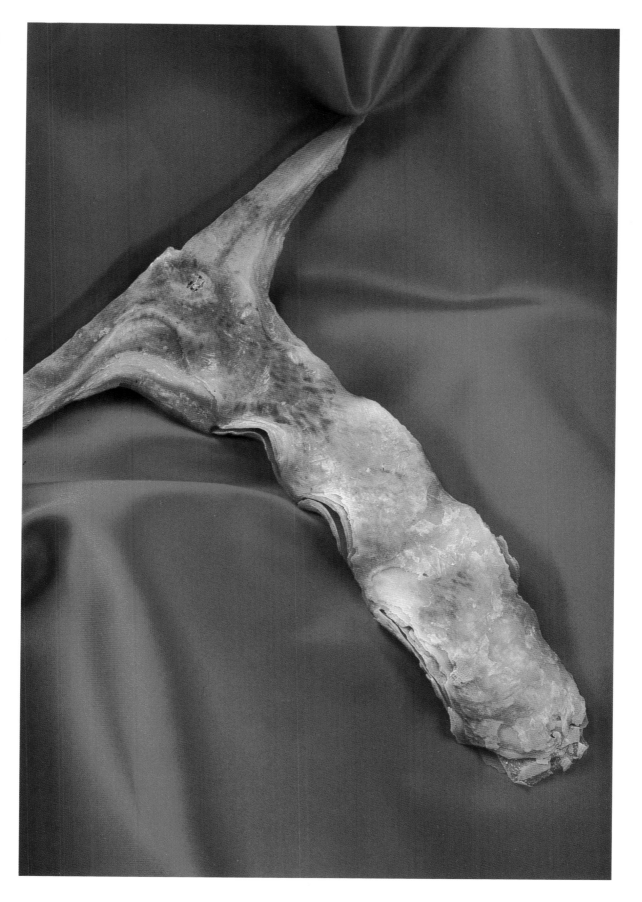

PLATE 180

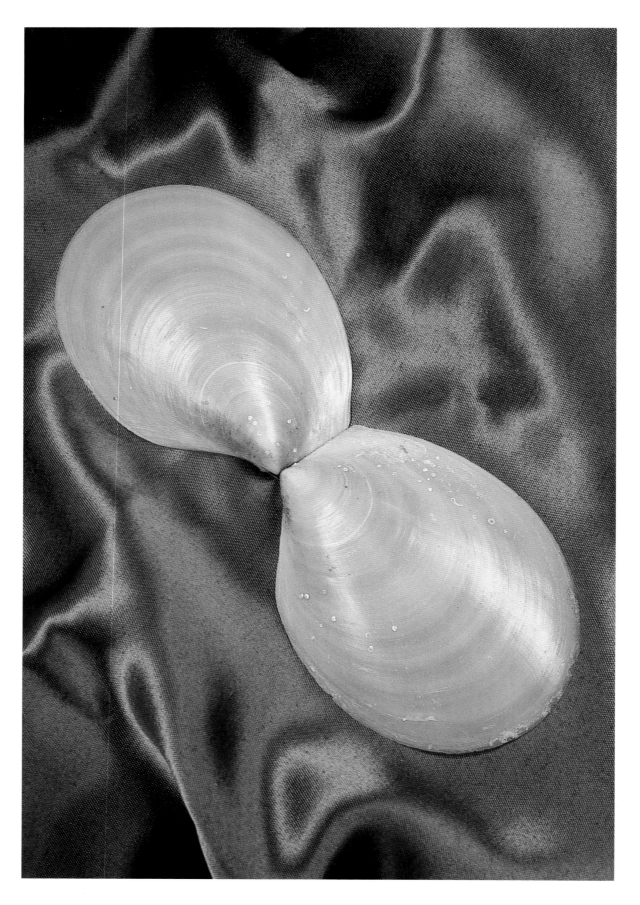

PLATE 181

PLATE 182

PLATE 183

PLATE 184

PLATE 185

PLATE 186

PLATE 187

PLATE 188

Family FIMBRIIDAE

Plate 189
Fimbria fimbriata (Linné, 1758)
COMMON BASKET LUCINA
Indian and Pacific Oceans
3 to 4 inches (7.5 to 10 cm)

The delicate surface sculpture of this Common Basket Lucina helps to stabilize the shell in the sandy bottom.

Family CHAMIDAE

Plate 190
Chama lazarus Linné, 1758
LAZARUS JEWEL BOX
Tropical Indian and Pacific Oceans
2 to 3 inches (5 to 7.5 cm)

These bivalves live attached to hard bottoms from below the tide line to depths of 165 feet (50 meters). Like the spines of thorny oysters, the broad foliations of the shell edge serve to increase the effective volume of the shell, and to provide holdfasts for encrusting organisms.

Family CARDIIDAE

Plate 191
Cardium costatum Linné, 1758
GREAT RIBBED COCKLE
Western Africa
3 to 4 inches (7.5 to 10 cm)

These large, nearly spherical bivalves live buried just beneath the surface of subtidal mud flats. Being relatively slow burrowers, these animals rely on their broad ribs to stabilize their position within the substrate.

Plate 192
Corculum cardissa Linné, 1758
TRUE HEART COCKLE
Tropical Indian and Pacific Oceans
1 to 2 inches (2.5 to 5 cm)

Heart Cockles lie on the surface of shallow sandy bottoms. Their shells contain translucent areas that admit light for the algae that grow within the tissues of this bivalve and supplement its diet. The shell has become flattened and laterally expanded to maximize the area exposed to sunlight.

Family TRIDACNIDAE

Plate 193
Tridacna crocea Lamarck, 1819
CROCUS GIANT CLAM
Southwestern Pacific to Japan
3 to 4 inches (7.5 to 10 cm)

Larvae of giant clams settle on coral and become attached by means of a byssus. By rocking the shell along the plane of the valves, they gradually abrade a niche into the coral.

Plate 194
Tridacna squamosa Lamarck, 1819
FLUTED GIANT CLAM
Tropical Indian and Pacific Oceans
4 to 12 inches (10 to 30 cm)

Like the corals among which they live, giant clams have developed an unusual association with unicellular algae called zooxanthillae. The algae grow within the tissues of the greatly expanded mantle edge and supplement the diet of the giant clam.

Family SOLENIDAE

Plate 195
Solen brevis Gray in Hanley, 1842
BRIEF JACKKNIFE CLAM
Southwestern Pacific and Indian Oceans
3 to 4 inches (7.5 to 10 cm)

Members of this family live in vertical burrows beneath the surface of intertidal marine and estuarine sand and mud flats. The animals are well adapted for rapid burrowing. The edges of the mantle are fused to form a tubular mantle cavity. The long, muscular foot operates like a piston, plunging into the soft bottom, expanding and drawing the shell behind it. Laid on its side on the surface of the sand, a large specimen is capable of completely burying itself in less than a minute.

Family TELLINIDAE

Plate 196
Phylloda foleacea (Linné, 1758)
FOLIATED TELLIN
Southwestern Pacific Ocean
2 to 3 inches (5 to 7.5 cm)

Unlike most burrowing bivalves, many tellins live with their shells in a horizontal position. This is reflected by a slight asymmetry in their valves, the right, or upper valve being slightly flatter. The inhalant and exhalant siphons are separate and operate independently. The exhalant siphon is shorter, and extends to the sand surface directly above the edge of the shell. The longer inhalant siphon scans the sand surface like a vacuum cleaner hose, sucking up organic debris and small organisms upon which the tellin feeds.

Family DONACIDAE

Plate 197
Hecuba scortum (Linné, 1758)
LEATHER DONAX
Southwestern Pacific and Indian Oceans
2 inches (5 cm)

Most members of this family live in the surf zone of sandy beaches, and travel up and down the beach with the tides. The animals are frequently exposed as the waves churn the sand, and rely on their large, powerful foot to rebury themselves in a matter of seconds. The shell has an enlarged, wedge-shaped anterior region to accommodate the large foot and to facilitate burrowing.

Family GLOSSIDAE

Plate 198
Meiocardia moltkiana (Spengler, 1783)
MOLTKE'S HEART CLAM
East Indies and Philippines
1 to 1.5 inches (2.5 to 4 cm)

This species illustrates most clearly that the shells of bivalves consist of two coiled valves, each a mirror image of the other.

Family VENERIDAE

Plate 199
Pitar dione (Linné, 1758)
ROYAL COMB VENUS
West Indies
1.5 inches (4 cm)

The spines are limited to the posterior portion of the shell of this burrowing species, and are directed toward the sand surface. They surround the animal's siphons, and presumably protect them from grazing by fish and other predators.

Plate 200
Lioconcha castrensis (Linné, 1758)
CAMP PITAR VENUS
Tropical Indian and Pacific Oceans
1.5 inches (4 cm)

This shallowly burrowing species lives in sand flats. The animal inserts its foot into the sand and rocks the axe-blade-like edge of the shell into the substrate by alternate contractions of anterior and posterior sets of muscles.

Family PHOLADIDAE

Plate 201
Barnea dilatata (Souleyet, 1843)
DILATED FALSE ANGEL WING
Eastern Indian Ocean
3 to 4 inches (7.5 to 10 cm)

Although the shells of species in this family are extremely thin and delicate, they are used to burrowing through such substrates as clay, peat and wood, in which the animals live.

Plate 202
Jouannetia cumingii (Sowerby, 1849)
CUMING'S JOUANNETIA
Western Pacific Ocean
0.8 inch (2 cm)

This nearly spherical shell lives in shallow burrows excavated in coral.

Family PANDORIDAE

Plate 203
Pandora punctata Conrad, 1837
PUNCTATE PANDORA
Northeastern Pacific Ocean
1.5 inches (4 cm)

These bivalves lie on their side on the surface of sandy and muddy bottoms in calm waters. The shells are therefore asymmetrical. The bottom valve is deep and concave, the upper valve may be either flat or slightly concave.

Family CUSPIDARIIDAE

Plate 204
Cuspidaria rostrata (Spengler, 1793)
ROSTRATE CUSPIDARIA
Northern and western Atlantic Ocean
1 inch (2.5 cm)

These unusual bulb-shaped bivalves are carnivores. The gill has been reduced to a flat, muscular diaphragm which, when contracted, creates a sudden powerful vacuum at the constricted siphonal tube that sucks small crustaceans and worms into the mantle cavity.

Family VERTICORDIIDAE

Plate 205
Halicardissa perplicata (Dall, 1890)
PURPLISH HALICARDISSA
Pacific Ocean
1.5 inch (4 cm)

Like many animals that live at great depths (5,900 feet/1,800 meters) these bivalves are carnivores. Their flat, muscular gill pumps water rapidly and sporadically through the mantle cavity. Unlike cuspidarias, verticordiids have a broad inhalant siphon with long papillae extending from its edge.

Family CLAVIGELLIDAE

Plates 206/207
Penicillus penis (Linné, 1758)
COMMON WATERING POT
Indian Ocean
5 to 6 inches (12.5 to 15 cm)

These unusual bivalves begin life with a normal, bivalved shell that eventually becomes incorporated into a long, shell tube. The tube is buried vertically in mud, with only the foliated tip that surrounds the siphons remaining above the surface. The buried anterior end is surrounded by a flange-like anchor, and contains many thin, downwardly directed tubules. This end of the tube (plate 207) resembles a shower head or the spout of a watering can.

PLATE 189

PLATE 190

PLATE 191

PLATE 192

PLATE 193

PLATE 194

PLATE 195

PLATE 196

PLATE 197

PLATE 198

PLATE 199

PLATE 200

PLATE 202

PLATE 201

PLATE 203

PLATE 204

PLATE 205

PLATE 206

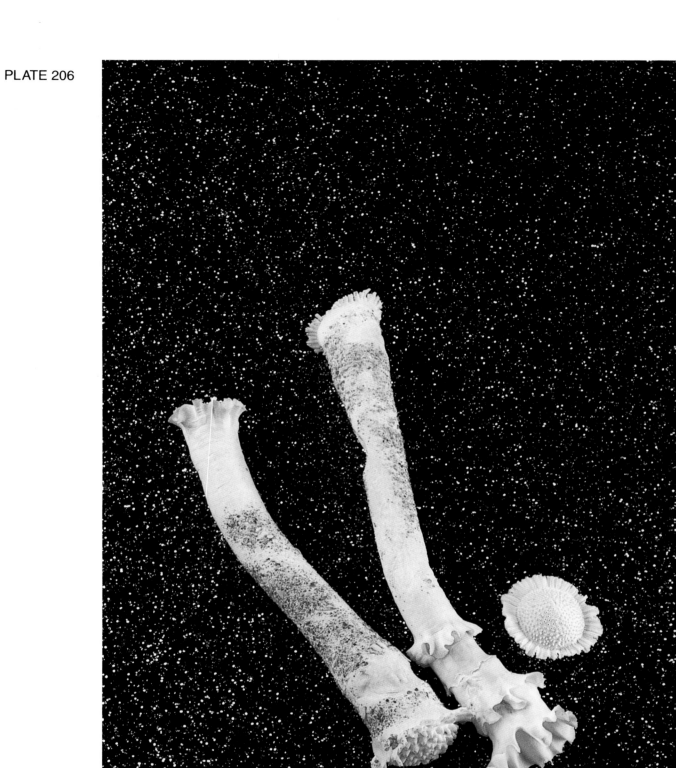

PLATE 207

CLASS

SCAPHOPODA

Family DENTALIIDAE

Plate 208
Dentalium longitrorsum Reeve, 1842
[*tan*]
ELONGATE TUSK
Tropical Indian and Pacific Oceans
3 to 4 inches (7.5 to 10 cm)

Dentalium aprinum Linné, 1766
[*greenish*]
BOAR'S TUSK
Tropical Indian and Pacific Oceans
2 inches (5 cm)

Dentalium lubricatum Sowerby, 1860
[*white*]
LUBRICATED TUSK
Australia
2.5 inches (6 cm)

The last of the major groups or classes of mollusks to evolve, the tusk shells are highly adapted for burrowing in sandy bottoms below tidal levels and feeding on foraminiferans and other protozoans. There is little variation among the approximately 350 known species.

Plate 209
Dentalium floridense Henderson, 1920
FLORIDA TUSK
Southeastern Florida and the West Indies
2 to 2.5 inches (5 to 6 cm)

Tusk shells range in size from a fraction of an inch to over 6 inches (a few millimeters to over 15 cm) in length. All live by burrowing vertically or obliquely in the sand, with the narrow ends of the shell at or near the surface. Although the shell is a tube with openings at both ends, water for respiration enters and leaves through the smaller orifice.

Plate 210
Dentalium elephantinum (Linné, 1758)
ELEPHANT TUSK
Japan to the Philippines
3 inches (7.5 cm)

and *Dentalium formosum* Adams and Reeve, 1850
FORMOSAN TUSK
Eastern Asia
2 inches (5 cm)

These two species are among the few tusk shells to have color. The vast majority are pure white or glassy. The presence and strength of raised longitudinal cords along the outer surfaces of some species may be correlated with the grain size of the sediments in which these tusk shells live.

PLATE 208

PLATE 209

PLATE 210

PHOTOGRAPHER'S STATEMENT

I've always been interested in natural forms. I am amazed by objects like seashells, because the sole purpose of their design is survival. It fascinates me how each aesthetic detail can be appreciated for its specific survival function as well as its perceived beauty.

As a photographer, I find it visually pleasing to explore these shapes, colors and textures. It is exciting to discover and capture on film the moment when, through an unusual angle or method of lighting, the object reveals a visual aspect that had been hidden previously. Shells are very photogenic. Many photographers have rendered varied interpretations of shells ranging from erotic to minimalistic. These renderings tell us as much about the photographer as they do about the shell.

I see a bit of the mystery of life in the diversity of shape and form of shells. To me, the enigma of a natural object rests in its ability to portray different things to different people. What people find visually pleasing has more to do with what they bring to an image than what the image contains.

I believe most people would choose order over disorder. But it is the job of the visual artist to walk the fine line between creating an image so ordered it is devoid of mystery or rendering one so complex it leaves viewers baffled. This is like life itself. An existence with no surprises soon proves boring; one that is chaotic may be unendurably stressful. That point of balance depends solely on individual taste, is purely subjective, difficult to pinpoint and in a constant state of flux.

For me, the creative process is at once meditative and intuitive. I find I am usually the most productive when I'm the least self-conscious. It is at these moments the element of surprise works its magic. The most challenging thing for me is combining elements in a new and unusual way to create a fresh eye, a new way of seeing.

I was privileged, while working on this book to have the world's finest collection of seashells at my disposal. It's easy to assume that these magnificent specimens would be simple to shoot. This is one of the most common misunderstandings about photography and its process. Sometimes it's the seemingly unexceptional that is rendered extraordinary and the exceptional that appears mundane.

In order to devise a background that would compliment each shell, I experimented with surfaces as varied as marble, wood, plastic, fabric and paper. Often my final choice was based on a feeling of appropriateness rather than any hard and fast rules.

I was blessed with good editors who gave me the artistic freedom to indulge my whims. All of us began the project convinced this book was not intended to be a compendium of shells but, rather, a window enhancing our knowledge of the natural world. With that in mind, and over 600 specimens shipped to my studio from the Smithsonian Institution, I set out to tell a visual story.

For those interested in the nuts and bolts of the type of equipment used, there is no great mystery here. All photographs were taken with a Nikon F3 camera with a 55 macro lens and Kodachrome 64 was the film of choice.

Murray Alcosser
New York, New York

Plate 211
Charonia Tritonis (Linné, 1758)
TRUMPET TRITON
Tropical Indian and Pacific Oceans
12 to 18 inches (30 to 45 cm)

PLATE 211